HIMSELF!

D1477885

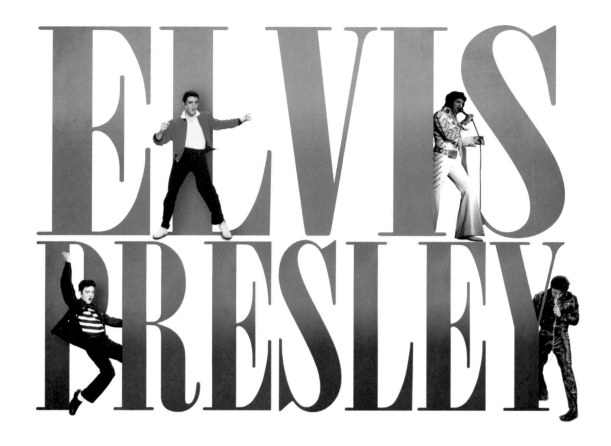

# ELVIS PRESLEY

## Love Me Tender

Written by
Carolyn McHugh

sona
BOOKS

## sona
### BOOKS

First published in the UK 2022 by Sona Books an imprint of Danann Media Publishing Ltd

**CAT NO: SON0497**
**Photography courtesy of**

**Getty images:**

| | | |
|---|---|---|
| ullstein bild | Terry O'Neill | GAB Archive/Redferns |
| CBS Photo Archive | National Archives / Handout | Sunset Boulevard/Corbis |
| Michael Ochs Archives / Handout | Fotos International | Paramount Pictures/Sunset Boulevard/Corbis |
| Bettmann | RB/Redferns | Lee Lockwood |
| Hulton Archive / Stringer | Steve Morley | Keystone Features/Hulton Archive |
| GAB Archive | Archive Photos / Stringer | Michael Ochs Archives / Stringer |
| Movie Poster Image Art | Ben Mancuso | Silver Screen Collection |
| Sunset Boulevard | Memphis Brooks Museum/Michael Ochs Archives | John Kobal Foundation |
| Don Cravens | Keystone Features/Hulton Archive | Magma Agency |

**Alamy images:**

• United Archives GmbH     • Everett Collection Inc
• PictureLux / The Hollywood Archive     • Alain Le Garsmeur Elvis Presley Collection

Other images **Wiki Commons**

Book layout & design Darren Grice at Ctrl-d
Copy editor Juliette O'Neill

Made in EU.
**ISBN: 978-1-912918-60-7**

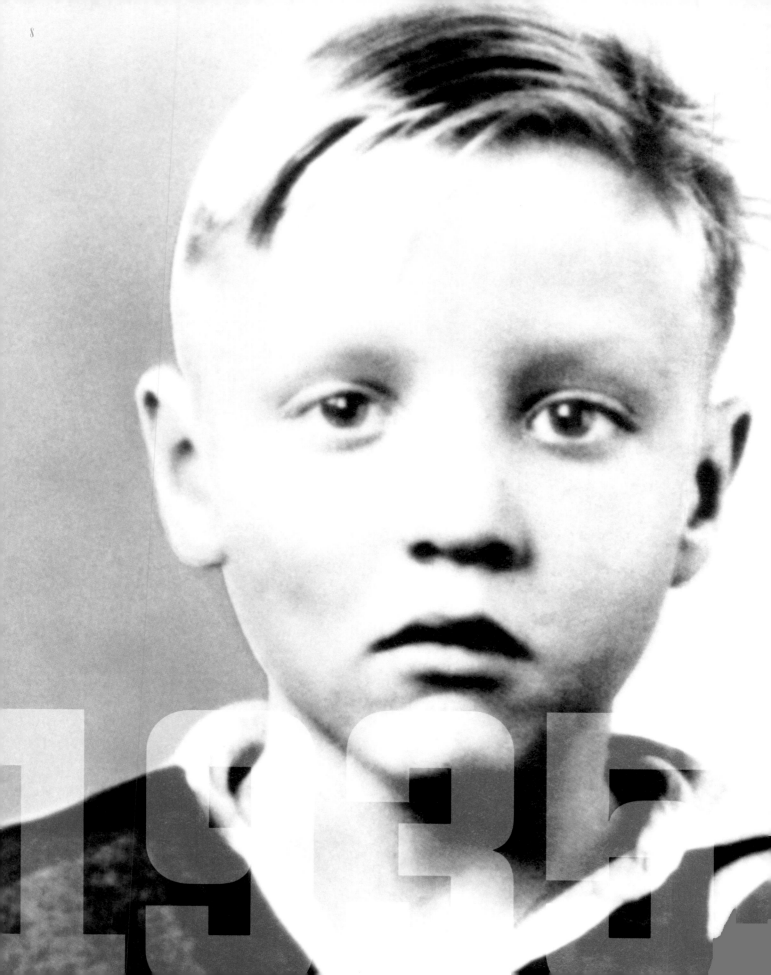

# The twin who lived

Just moments after his birth in the early hours of 8 January 1935, Elvis Aaron Presley was at the centre of a drama. His twin brother Jesse was delivered stillborn, understandably devastating his young parents Gladys and Vernon.

Although unaware of the family's distress at the time, Elvis would be affected by the event for his entire life. Firstly, the loss of Jesse (sometimes recorded as 'Jessie') meant that his mother became incredibly anxious and overly attentive towards Elvis, now her only son. Secondly, Elvis was left to wonder about the relationship he might have had with his twin. Who knows, if Jesse had been around when Elvis became a star, he might have provided a much-needed anchor for his brother. Certainly, Elvis hated to be alone as an adult which is perhaps why he surrounded himself with cronies - in a search for the brotherly love he was missing. The question 'why me?' which puzzles many famous people was exacerbated for Elvis, who would wonder, not only 'why did I become famous?', but 'why was I the twin who lived?'.

He remained an only child. Gladys and Vernon were very young when he was born, Gladys aged 22 and Vernon just 18, so there was plenty of time for more children. One clue comes from a 1978 interview Vernon gave to *Good Housekeeping* magazine in the US, where he said; 'When Elvis was about ten years old…I can only say that God spoke to my heart and told me that Elvis was the only child we'd ever have and the only child we'd ever need. Elvis was a special gift who would fill our lives completely. Without little Jesse who was born dead, without the other children we'd hoped to have, we understood that we were an extraordinarily complete family circle.

'As soon as I realised that Elvis was meant to be an only child, I felt as though a burden was lifted. I never again wondered why we didn't have additional sons and daughters. It's hard to describe the feelings Elvis, his mother and I had for each other. Though we had friends and relatives, including my parents, the three of us formed our own private world.'

The family's 'private world' was however an extremely poor one, which might also have factored in the decision-making.

Their first very basic home in East Tupelo, Mississippi, stood on a dirt road and had no running water, no electricity and no bathroom or inside toilet. The property was known as a 'shotgun house' – so called because its two rooms were laid out in a straight line so that technically a gunshot could pass from the front to the back door without hitting anything.

Life was hard and there were times when the family had little to eat. Gladys would work picking cotton, first with baby Elvis lying beside her, then when he was older he would work by her side, helping her.

Then things got worse for the family. In 1938 when Elvis was three years old, Vernon, who did odd jobs including farm work and truck driving, was sent to prison for forging a cheque. The forgery was something Vernon said he had felt he had to do in order to put food on the table.

While Vernon was away, Gladys and Elvis were evicted after Gladys was unable to pay the monthly $12 rent on their house. Mother and son had to move around, staying with family and at various boarding houses, until Vernon's release.

Things settled down and Elvis enrolled at East Tupelo Consolidated School in 1942, aged seven.

Despite their economic difficulties, there were certainly plenty of happy times for Elvis and his parents who were part of a large extended family, including his paternal grandmother Minnie Mae. Vernon and Gladys were also closely involved with their local church, The Assembly of God. The sound of hymns and gospel songs rang out around the house - Gladys had a good voice which her son had evidently inherited. Elvis became used to singing in church from a very young age. He also picked up some useful tips on performance - the uplifting effect a rousing church service could have on the congregation was certainly not lost on young Elvis, who would later incorporate some of that style, copied from black preachers and singers, into his performances.

Although his background was poor, Elvis found there were tremendous riches in the music world and would listen avidly to the radio, absorbing all sorts of rhythms and styles from country, blues and gospel. Programmes featuring singers such as Sister Rosetta Tharpe and Arthur "Big Boy" Crudup were popular choices and Elvis would also be sure to catch The Grand Ole Opry country show on a Saturday evening.

He would eventually blend all these different influences together in the unique vocal style which made him famous. Yet at the time there were few clues that Elvis would become a star. He was quite a shy boy, well behaved and deferential, keen to please his mother who prized good manners.

By all accounts he was an 'average' student, something which must have disappointed Gladys who viewed education as his passport out of their impoverished life. Little did she know that in fact it was the guitar he received as an 11th birthday present that would signal his exit route.

The story goes that he asked for a bicycle but got a guitar because it was cheaper. Many of the family's relatives played and were able to help him learn some basic chords. Playing guitar did not come to him as easily as singing did, but he persevered with his beginner's instruction book, and later, a pastor, Frank Smith helped him as well. His guitar became his new best friend – although he would later say

that he was really a simple rhythm player, leaving the more complicated guitar work to more skilled hands. But he would sit and play in the house for hours, encouraged by Gladys in particular.

Meanwhile his parents continued to work to better themselves. First, they moved out of East Tupelo to neighbouring Tupelo itself. But when nothing worked out for them there, the family made another, more ambitious, move by heading to the big city of Memphis, Tennessee. Here, as part of America's New Deal housing programme, the Presley's were eventually able to move into a decent, affordable apartment, which was bigger than anywhere they had lived before.

Elvis was 13 years old when he arrived in Memphis in 1948. The place was so different from Tupelo that it was almost the equivalent of moving to Paris. Memphis was much more affluent and cultured than his birthplace, full of life, and opportunities.

The city, with the powerful Mississippi river running through it, had attracted lots of new people from the southern states seeking better opportunities after World War Two. Key for Elvis, there was a big entertainment district, full of the sounds the city's new citizens had brought with them.

Elvis found that his horizons expanded, and his fortunes improved. His parents gave him what money they could for records and trips to music concerts. He loved going into central Memphis - the sounds, the sights and the bright lights excited him, and he became a willing student of music as he visited the clubs on Beale Street at the heart of the scene. He had eclectic taste and picked up influences from all around him, witnessing for example the talent of entertainers such as B.B. King and Rufus Thomas and noting their powerful connection with audiences.

Slowly he began to put together a version of himself which the world would come to know as 'Elvis'. He let his hair grow longer, formed it into a quiff and added sideburns as soon as he could. His childhood shyness seemed to have evaporated as he grew to find his place in life and now Elvis was happy to stand out from the crowd.

Although at his new school, Hume High School, he had found himself at the bottom of the social pecking order at first. Classmates would mock the way he talked and daydreamed. But all that was to change when Elvis entered the school minstrel show. He gave a knockout rendition of *'Till I Walk With You Again'* which stunned his schoolmates – suddenly they understood what he was all about and where his talents lay.

'It was amazing how popular I became after that,' Elvis said later. It was his first taste of the heady nectar of adulation. Yet, within months, school was over. Elvis graduated high school on 3 June 1953, the first person in his family ever to do so. It was a proud night for him and his parents.

But what next for a poor boy from Memphis? Continuing lack of funds meant going on to college wasn't an option – he needed to earn some money. And in fact, he was keen to help his parents by bringing some extra cash into the home and to make his mother proud. His first job on an assembly line didn't last long, then he joined Crown Electric as an apprentice electrician for $3 an hour where his duties included driving a truck and helping the electricians pull wires.

It was while he was on the road that he began driving past the Memphis Recording Service, owned by Sam Phillips who was setting up a new label called Sun Records. Things were suddenly about to happen and, as it turned out, the closest young Elvis would get to qualifying as an electrician would be when he got on stage and began generating power of his own…

*Young Elvis at school Circa 1947*

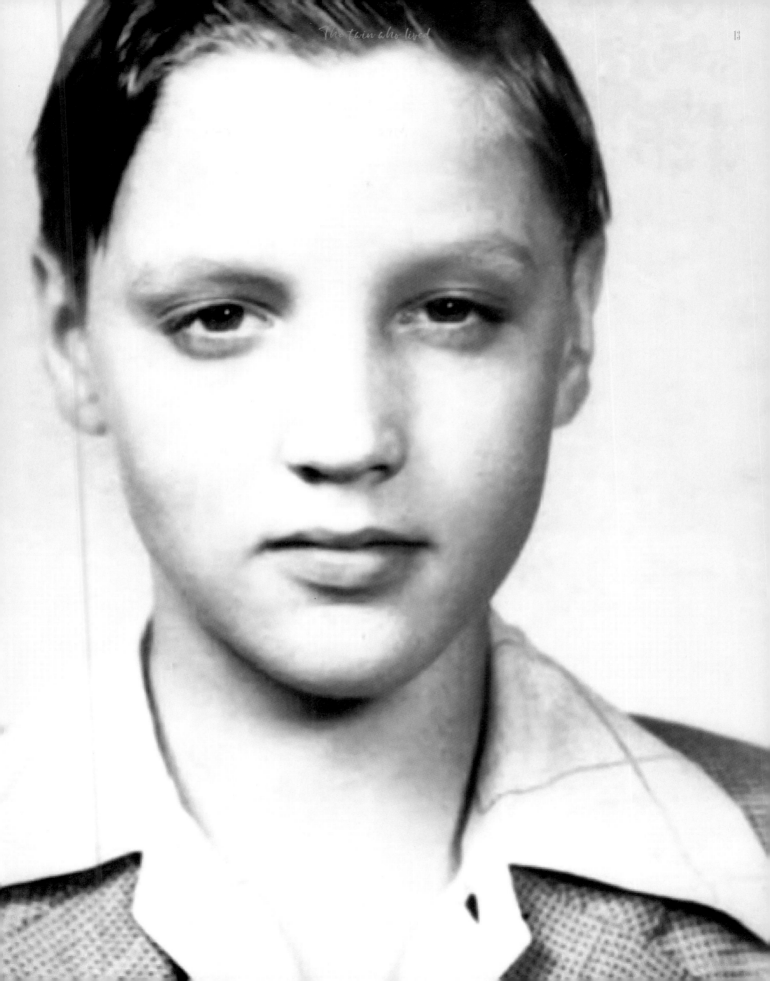

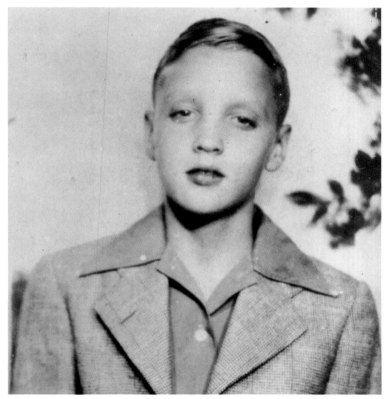

ABOVE

Elvis & parents outside of their home in Tupelo, Mississippi

ABOVE LEFT

Two year old Elvis Presley poses for a family portrait with his parents Vernon Presley and Gladys Presley in 1937 in Tupelo, Mississippi

LEFT

Elvis at around 12 years old

OPP. PAGE

Portrait of Elvis Presley, circa 1953/1954

16

1954.

# The boy who would be King

1955

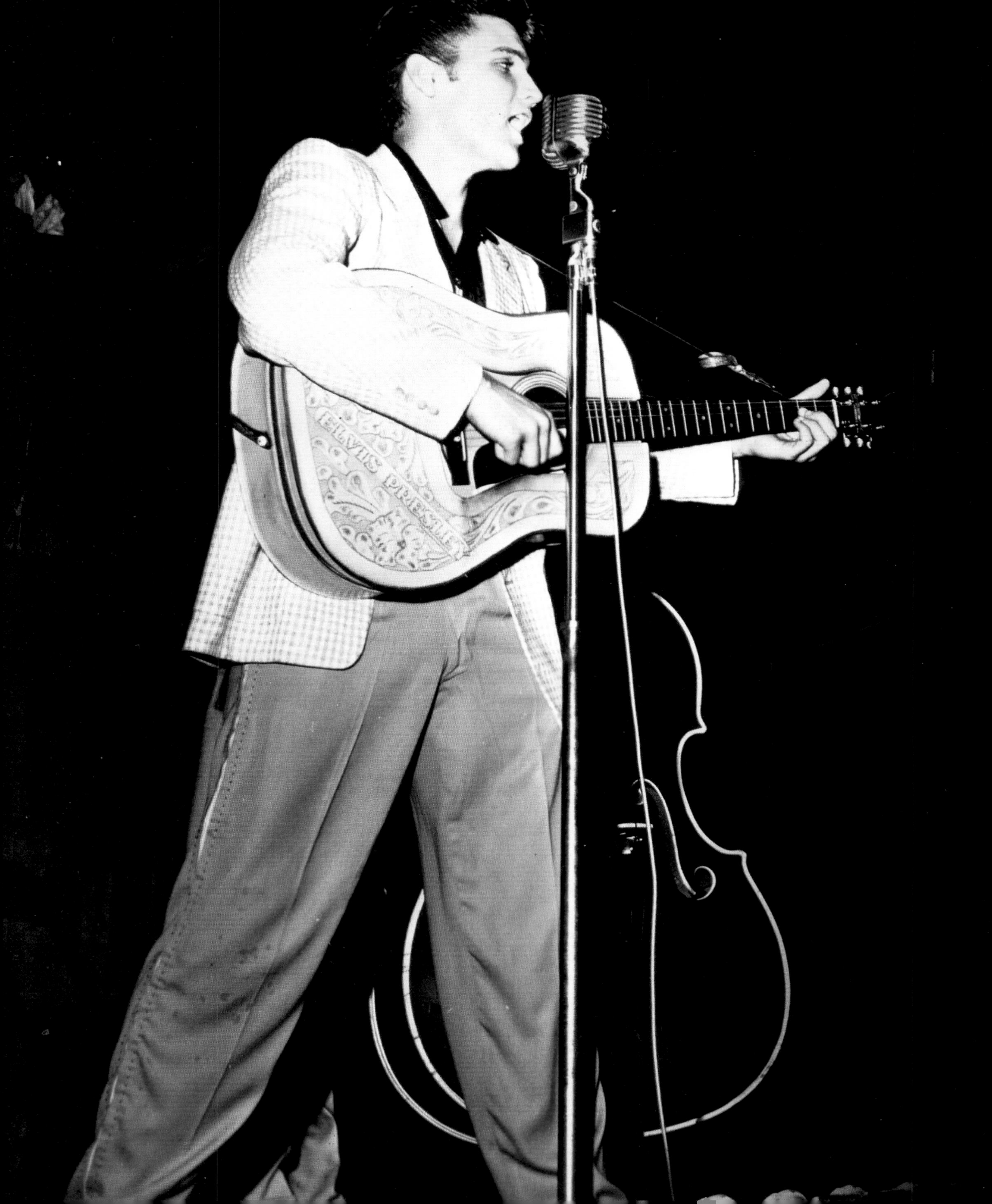
ELVIS PRESLEY

Elvis knew that Sun Records' supremo Sam Phillips was looking for raw talent, something different, and was not deterred in anyway by a person's background, colour or social status. He eventually plucked up the courage to go inside and paid $4 to record a song. The story goes that he did so as a present for his mother, although if that were really the case, he could have done so more cheaply elsewhere such as in a local five and dime store. More likely he wanted the big time.

The songs chosen for this first record were the ballads 'My Happiness' and That's When Your Heartaches Begin' which he recorded on the two-sides of a 10in acetate disc, accompanying himself on guitar. Although this early recording showcased many of the qualities of his singing which contributed to his eventual success, such as the vulnerability and emotional charge in his voice, there wasn't an instant breakthrough by any means. For about a year Elvis would drop into the studios to sing when he could and make occasional appearances in venues around the town without any notable success.

What he didn't know was that he had a big fan at the studio, Marion Keisker, a radio producer who worked part time with Sam at Sun Records. Having made a note that Elvis was 'a good ballad singer', she told Sam about the young man she had met and in June 1954 Sam Phillips called him in for a real audition to make a commercial recording.

Elvis was asked to sing a new song that Phillips had been given called 'Without You'. Sam sat watching for some three hours, asking Elvis to sing it over again in different styles. Elvis performed the number in every way he knew, but left the studio feeling unsure about how he had done. He was relieved to receive a call inviting him back in for a second audition.

Although nothing from that first audition had been particularly exciting, Sam felt he could do something with Elvis, so this time he wanted to team him up with two other musicians, guitarist Scotty Moore and double bass player Bill Black. The three played together for a few hours as Sam listened but gave little in the way of encouraging feedback. Elvis was rather unnerved and rattled as he felt things weren't going especially well. He was nervous and stiff and, probably as an attempt to loosen himself up during a break in proceedings, he began singing an up-tempo version of Arthur Crudup's 1946 blues song That's Alright (Mama), delivering it at almost twice the speed of the original. Scotty and Bill joined in, jamming along although they didn't know the song themselves. Sam liked what he overheard and began to sound enthusiastic for the first time during the whole session and set about recording it.

Scotty and Bill – much more experienced musicians – knew that something special had happened in the studio that night with Elvis, although they weren't sure exactly what it would mean. The sound was so different, neither blues nor country but a unique fusion of both styles with a dash of bluegrass thrown in the mix. With their help Elvis had come up with a vibrant new sound of his very own which was to turn his life, and the music world, upside down. Rock historians believe the number to be the first real rock and roll record.

As Scotty Moore describes it; 'It was at least 10 o'clock, it was getting late, we were about ready to go to the house cos it was still just an audition. And Elvis stood up and started playing his guitar and singing That's Alright and Bill started slapping his bass and playing along with him. I had never heard the song, Bill had never heard it, and I took the guitar and started playing, looking for something, we were just jamming.

'The door to the control room was open and Sam stuck his head out and said, "What are you guys

*Elvis on stage with his brand new Martin D-28 acoustic guitar. July 31, 1955 at Fort Homer Hesterly Armory in Tampa, Florida*

doing?" We said, "We're just goofing around" and he said; "Well just do it a little more". Cos the mikes weren't on or anything and he said "Let me go and turn the mikes on" or whatever and we got on the mike, went through it 2 or 3 times and that was it. Lord am I glad or am I sorry, I don't know!'

When Sam was happy at last, he gave the recorded demo to his friend DJ Dewey Phillips to play on his 'Red, Hot and Blue' radio show on the Memphis radio station WHBQ. His listeners loved it and the next day demand for the record was through the roof. The only hiccough was that there was no B side, so the trio hurriedly returned to the studio and recorded *'Blue Moon of Kentucky'* – a country song transformed by Elvis' vocal magic and Sam's ramping up of the pace.  A week later Sun Records had 6,000 advanced orders for the record.

No-one creates music in a vacuum, but sometimes there's a crossroads moment when something new is born. This had happened for Elvis, who had electrified the audience. Now with a hit record he needed to capitalise on this success. Prepared to do the hard work he hit the road with Scotty and Bill. One of their early gigs was at the Memphis Overton Park Shell amphitheatre as part of a programme featuring yodeller Slim Whitman. As they played they became increasingly aware of loud and wildly appreciative noise from the audience, particularly from the females at the front. Scotty later said that they realised it was because Elvis moved his legs to the rhythm. Although Elvis would always deny he was doing it deliberately, he was nevertheless aware of the effect it had.

With more money in his pocket than he'd ever had before, Elvis treated himself to a new guitar, a Martin D-18 which cost him $175 – an unimaginable extravagance just a few months before.

Throughout 1954 and 1955 bookings for the trio slowly increased in number. The three boys drove and slept in their car so the travelling and performance schedule was often gruelling.

Scotty Moore remembers those early days; 'Starting off like that, none of us had ever been on the road so number one you'd have an experience and then pretty soon you'd start to get tired and say will this never end. And yet tomorrow the next show will be better, there'll be a better show, there'll be more money, it'll be, you know, everything is supposed to go up. But we were just typical, like, I won't say like any other band that's out there but – we'd have our fusses and everything.

'We had a problem with Elvis when he was driving – he was a good driver, a very good driver – but for some reason he just could not read road signs. If you came to a fork in the road, well, he'd take the wrong one every time. But he was a good driver.'

Despite all the hard work, Elvis would later recall the time as a period of real happiness, remembered particularly whenever he sang *'That's Alright'* on stage which he did for the rest of his life. This time on tour also helped him to attain a depth of craft which is simply impossible to achieve any other way.

Before long an ambitious Sam Phillips secured the trio a dream gig – an appearance at the Grand Ole Opry in Nashville for a radio show. But sadly the audience wasn't ready for what Elvis had to offer and the performance didn't go down well. A member of management there advised the trio not to give up their day jobs which hurt Elvis so much that he would never perform there again.

In fact, the trio had given up their jobs and now worked together exclusively as The Blue Moon Boys, with Scotty as manager and Sam Phillips recording and promoting them.

Elvis, Scotty and Bill were a winning combination of rawness, vision and drive and by early 1955, were

*Performing at Brooklyn High School Auditorium October 20, 1955 in Cleveland, Ohio.*

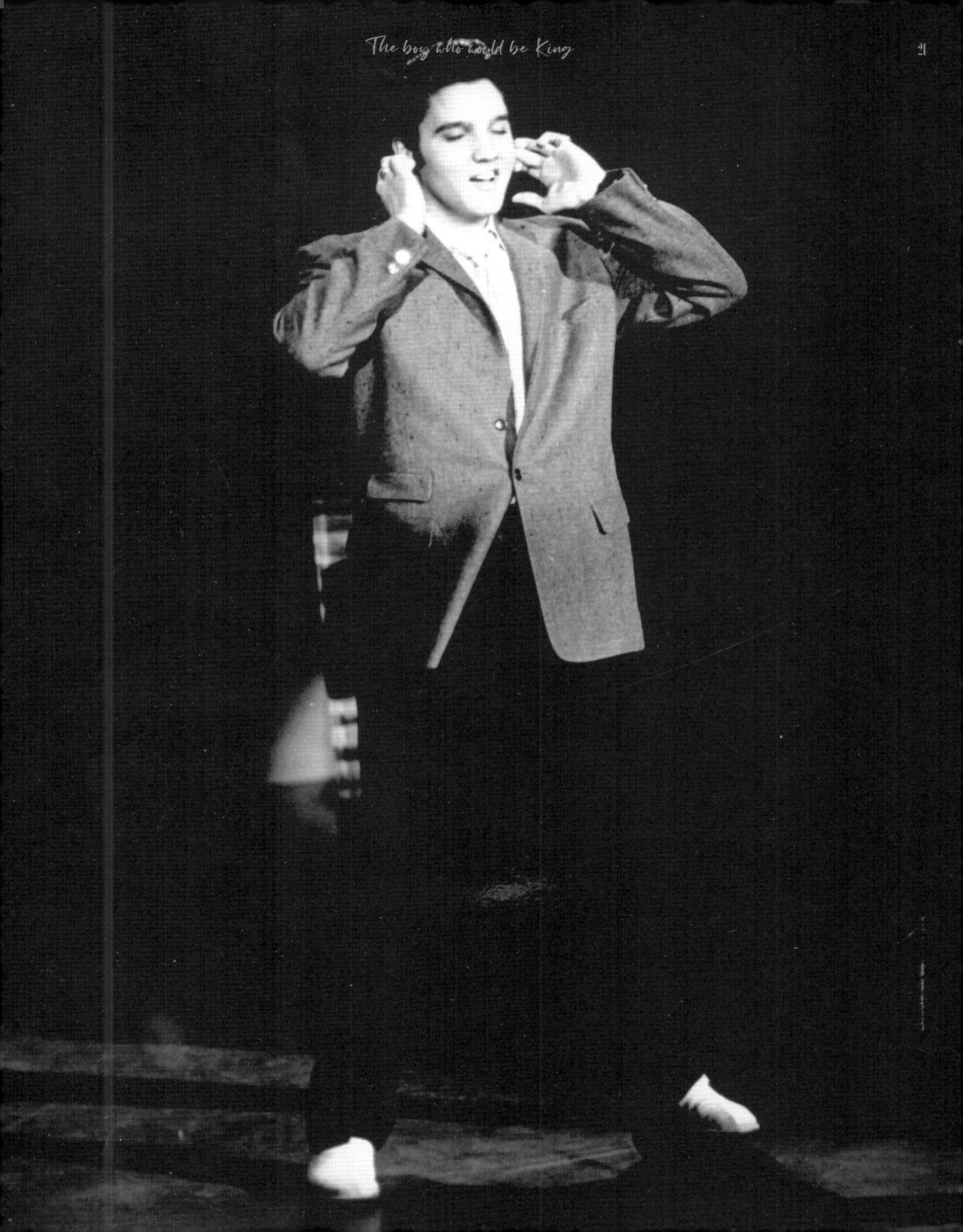

# Elvis and Sun Records

Elvis recorded at least 24 songs at Sun Studios in Memphis, Tennessee between 1953 and 1955. 10 of them (equating to five singles A and B sides) were released and are indicated with asterix)

**1953**

My Happiness

That's When Your Heartaches Begin

**1954**

I'll Never Stand in Your Way

It Wouldn't be the Same Without You

I Love You Because

That's Alright / Blue Moon of Kentucky*

Harbor Lights

Blue Moon

Tomorrow Night

I'll Never Let You Go (Little Darlin')

Satisfied

Good Rockin' Tonight / I Don't Care If The Sun Don't Shine*

Just Because

Milkcow Blues Boogie / You're A Heartbreaker*

**1955**

Baby Let's Play House / I'm Left, You're Right, She's Gone*

I Got a Woman

Tryin' to Get to You

I Forgot to Remember to Forget / Mystery Train *

When It Rains It Really Pours

# IN PERSON
## ELVIS
# PRESLEY
### and His
## ALL-STAR SHOW

## MULTNOMAH STADIUM
## MON., SEPT. 2nd—8:30 P. M.
## $1⁵⁰ – $2⁵⁰ – $3⁵⁰

## TICKETS NOW –
## J. K. GILL CO.
## S. W. 5th and Stark

# SUNDAY - FEB. 6
### TWO SHOWS ★ 3:00 p.m. & 8:00 p.m.
# AUDITORIUM
### MEMPHIS, TENN.

# FARON YOUNG
#### ★ "IF YOU AIN'T LOVIN"
# MARTHA CARSON
#### ★ BEAUTIFUL GOSPEL SINGER
# FERLIN HUSKEY
#### THE HUSHPUPPIES
### Doyle and Teddy
## WILBURN BROTHERS
### Plus... MEMPHIS' OWN
# ELVIS PRESLEY
### SCOTTY and BILL
#### He'll Sing "HEARTBEAKER" - "MILK COW BOOGIE"
# MANY MORE...

# MEMORIAL AUDITORIUM
## BUFFALO, NY. ★ 8:00 P.M.
# SAT., JAN. 21 - 1956

# ELVIS
### PRESLEY JORDANAIRES
### "Tickets $1.75 - All Seats Reserved"

# EAGLES NEST
### IN PERSON
### MEMPHIS OWN...
# ELVIS PRESLEY
### WITH SCOTTY & BILL
### ♪ SINGING ♪
#### ✳ "HEART BREAKER" ✳ "THATS ALL RIGHT"
#### ✳ "GOOD ROCKIN" ✳
### AS HEARD ON...
# WHBQ
## M.C. DEWEY PHILLIPS
### EXTRA ORDINARY MPHS D.J.

# Enter the Colonel

The name forever inextricably linked with Elvis Presley is that of his manager, Colonel Tom Parker. For better or worse, Parker made the decisions that steered Elvis's entire career.

For better, Parker was a marketing genius who struck unprecedented and lucrative contracts which made both men phenomenally rich. But 'for worse', Parker had little to no musical or artistic vision. He was just about the deals, the contracts and the bottom line. His determination to follow the money means that the world probably missed out on some magnificent music because Parker kept Elvis in film studios for too long.

Furthermore, Parker is also the reason why Elvis never toured outside America, save a few trips over the border to Canada in the mid-1950s. Had he done so he would have attracted huge audiences and made his overseas fans very happy. Considering that a world tour would also have made mountains of cash it's even more mysterious that Parker wouldn't have set this up – his love of money being legendary. So there had to be another reason.

There was. Parker was an illegal immigrant with no passport. And couldn't risk getting one for fear his secret would come out.

Parker's big secret didn't come out until the 1980s, after Elvis had died. He did not come from Virginia as he claimed, nor was Tom Parker his real name. He was in fact, born Andreas Cornelis (Dries) van Kuijk in the Netherlands on 26 June 1909 to a family of very modest means. After arriving in the States in 1929 by stowing away on a boat, he changed his name to Tom Parker.

The plot thickens thanks to a theory put forward by Parker's biographer Alanna Nash. In her book *The Colonel: The Extraordinary Story of Tom Parker and Elvis Presley* she writes that Parker's decision to leave the Netherlands, aged 20, was prompted by the fact that he was potentially a suspect in a murder there and, perhaps, left the country to avoid arrest.

Whatever the circumstances, Parker was determined to make the most of the opportunities which came his way once he'd made it to the United States. The country was thriving in the 1950s and its booming economy attracted more than two million immigrants all wanting to live 'the American Dream'.

Parker arrived with nothing but his wits, ambition and determination. After some time in the US army – his records are lost but he apparently was treated for psychosis following a period of solitary confinement as a punishment for desertion- he got a start in life by working as a 'carny' – American slang for a carnival worker.

Travelling circuses and carnivals were popular at the time and a good place for somebody to 'hide'. Parker did all sorts of jobs, for example demonstrating his entrepreneurial side when as an elephant groomer he made money on the side by selling their manure. He had probably gained his ability to work with animals when working at the stables run by his father back in Breda, Netherlands.

He reportedly also spent time as a dog catcher and pet cemetery founder. There are plenty of stories about him, but he was such a secretive person that many proved difficult to substantiate. His dancing chickens act for example may have been his first flirtation with the music business. Claiming to have chickens which danced whenever they heard country music, Parker actually made the birds hop around by turning on a steel hot plate, which unbeknownst to the audience formed the floor of their cage. The chickens were simply trying to avoid being burned.

The story may be apocryphal, but even so it illustrates the idea that no one would put such an antic beyond him. Parker was a larger than life character, noisy and capricious, fond of dressing in fine clothing and with a pretty high opinion of himself which belied his humble beginnings. In later life he became a friend to presidents and captains of industry who had no inkling that he had started out in America as a penniless immigrant.

Eventually Parker made his move out of carnivals and into the mainstream entertainment business by managing several country music singers. He would still use his 'carnival showman' skills to sell tickets and entice the crowds to see his acts perform.

Furthering his climb up the ladder, Parker gained a title. A singer he had got to know called Jimmie Davis was now running to become Governor of Louisiana and enlisted his help in his election campaign. Once Davies was installed as Governor, in 1948, he rewarded Parker for 'political services rendered' with the honorary title of 'Colonel' in the Louisiana State Militia. Parker revelled in the credibility this title bestowed upon him as it made his new Americanised persona complete.

Now styling himself as Colonel Tom Parker, he began enjoying some genuine success, making a good living by managing popular country singers such as Eddy Arnold and Hank Snow who became big names. But then came an opportunity to move up into a different league entirely – he spotted Elvis and knew he'd hit the jackpot.

Elvis and the Blue Moon Boys had got themselves a gig on a Hank Snow tour, and Snow introduced them to Parker, with whom he had set up a music promotions company.

To say that Parker was savvy doesn't quite cover it. He's been described as everything from a scoundrel to a genius – he was undoubtedly a smart marketing supremo, a brilliant promoter and a man with an eye for the main chance. As soon as he saw Elvis, he recognised his potential to be the figurehead of a new kind of music – rock and roll – and felt that this new talent and his innovative sound would soon eclipse Eddy and Hank and all that had gone before. A born entrepreneur, The Colonel, as Elvis always called him, was determined to get in on the action and quickly outmanoeuvred everyone in his

quest to work with Elvis. He didn't want Scotty and Bill, and eventually he shook off Hank as well.

Initially Parker provided the team around Elvis with some welcome support around bookings and promotions as they struggled to handle his burgeoning success. Then once he had a foot in the door, Parker worked hard to become indispensable and by 1955 had gained the title and position of 'special advisor' to Elvis.

But that was never going to be enough for him. Next to be supplanted was Sam Phillips and Sun Records. Parker persuaded Sam Phillips to sell him his contract with Elvis so that he could sign him up with a new record label – RCA Victor. Although Sam was sorry to see Elvis go, he had always had his best interests at heart and understood that, going forward, Elvis would need the backing of a bigger label to achieve national success.

Since signing with Sun Records in 1954, Elvis's early recordings had brought him some regional success in the South, from Florida to Texas – but there was still a big market to break. For his part, Elvis realised that he needed to make the move to further his career and that he needed Parker's knowledge of the business world, and the advent of television to help him breakthrough to national and international audiences.

Sam released Elvis from his Sun contract for $35,000 – an unprecedented amount of money at the time - and Elvis officially became an RCA artist on 21 November 1955.

Parker's final move was to oust and replace Elvis's manager Bob Neal, the Memphis radio personality who had taken over from Scotty in January 1955.

As well as being Elvis's manager, Parker fully seized the role of mentor and quasi father figure. He dropped his other artists and decided to devote himself entirely to Elvis. The decision was another smart move – Elvis was about to conquer the world.

# *Did you know?*

As well as launching the career of Elvis Presley, Sam Phillips signed other successful artists including Jerry Lee Lewis, Roy Orbison, Carl Perkins and Johnny Cash. Sam sold Sun Records in 1969 and used some of the money he raised to invest in the Holiday Inn chain of hotels

Jerry Lee Lewis, Carl Perkins, Elvis Presley and Johnny Cash as
"The Million Dollar Quartet" Dec 4, 1956, Memphis, Tennessee

LEFT _____

Elvis Presley with his manager Colonel Tom Parker pose in front of a picture of the RCA Victor dog in circa 1957 in Memphis, Tennessee

ABOVE _____

Colonel Tom Parker circa 1955

# Becoming Elvis

Now a protégé of RCA, one of the world's largest recording companies, Elvis' apprenticeship was over.  As part of the new record deal brokered by Parker, Elvis had earned a US$5,500 cash advance and was on five per cent royalties.  Additionally, Parker sorted out a contract with renowned music publishers Hill and Range, which set up a separate firm called Elvis Presley Music, Inc which allowed Elvis and Parker to share ownership of songs bought by Hill and Range for him to record. This would make both men further vast amounts of money.

Gripped by the excitement of such a glittering future, Elvis had no hesitation in going along with all Parker's plans. But he was still a minor, aged 21 and so his father Vernon had to sign the contracts on his behalf.

In January 1956 Elvis and the band arrived in Nashville to start recording his first album for RCA. It was to be called simply 'Elvis Presley'. Despite signing him, RCA executives were nervous about the new singer and his new genre and style and so brought in some musicians and singers of their own to boost the sound. Scotty and Bill, who were still backing him, were joined by guitarist Chet Atkins and pianist Floyd Cramer, along with backing singers The Jordanaires vocal quartet.  The aim was to recreate the Sun Records sound, and three microphones were employed so that Elvis could move around as he sang.

The second track recorded during those early RCA sessions never made it on to the album but gave Elvis his first smash hit – this was Heartbreak Hotel.

Elvis had first been offered the song the year before by its writers Tommy Durden and Mae Boren Axton. Legend goes that its lyrics had been inspired by a newspaper article about the suicide of a young man who jumped from a hotel window. The song was certainly gloomy and other singers had turned it down, including the Wilburn Brothers who thought it was 'strange and almost morbid'.

Elvis however thought differently and, recognising the song's worth, he chose it as his first RCA single. It was released on 27 January 1956 and Elvis sang it live when he made his first networked television appearance on *Stage Show* that same month. The increasing popularity of TV during the 1950s

## The Jordanaires

The Jordanaires, billed as Elvis's backing vocalists, went on to work with Elvis for the next 14 years, both in the studio and for live appearances, as well as featuring in some of his films and many television shows. The quartet, comprising Gordon Stoker, Neal Matthews, Hoyt Hawkins and Hugh Jarrett originally formed as a gospel group in 1948.

Presley portrait in 1956 in Memphis, Tennessee

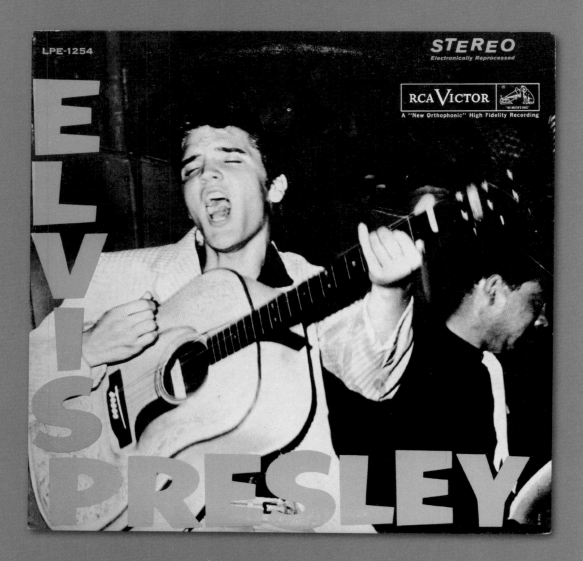

## Elvis Presley

His self-titled first album was released in March 1956. The iconic cover has gone on to become a classic, most famously aped by The Clash on their *London Calling* album of 1979. The rights to the tapes made during Elvis' time at Sun Studios had transferred to RCA Victor as part of the new contract with the sale of his contract, so five previously unreleased Sun songs, asterixed right, were added to the numbers recorded during the first RCA sessions.

The album went on to become the first rock and roll album to sell a million copies and is still regularly featured on 'greatest ever' album lists.

### Track list

Blue Suede Shoes
I'm Counting on You
I Got a Woman
One-Sided Love Affair
I Love You Because*
Just Because*
Tutti Frutti
Trying to Get to You*
I'm Gonna Sit Right Down and Cry Over You
I'll Never Let You Go (Little Darlin') *
Blue Moon*
Money Honey

was perfectly timed for the rise of Elvis and he made several appearances during early 1956, including more on *Stage Show* and then on *The Milton Berle* show.  Propelled by such national exposure *Heartbreak Hotel* gave Elvis his breakthrough hit, first number one single and first million-seller, topping the Billboard 100 chart for seven weeks, the Cashbox singles chart for six weeks and the Country and Western Chart for 17 weeks. It also made number three on the R&B chart.

Formerly a minor regional celebrity, Elvis had now arrived on the national stage. As well as propelling Elvis to instant stardom, the song made an incredible impact on many of the mega-star musicians who would follow in his wake, including The Beatles. Paul McCartney described the recording as nothing less than the most important artistic creation of the modern era, while John Lennon famously mooted the thought that; "Without Elvis, there would be no Beatles".

Yet his first hit single wasn't on his forthcoming album. At that time the singles market was much more important and the 'best songs' were singles, not album tracks.

However, there were plenty more good songs on the album; including his cover of the Carl Perkins hit *Blue Suede Shoes*, which was to become something of a signature song.

Following its release on 13 March 1956 it went to the top of the charts. In the 1950s an album was considered successful if it sold 10,000 copies - *Elvis Presley* sold 30,000 and has gone on to sell millions. The cover had his name written large in lurid pink and green over a black and white photograph of him in full performance mode, guitar in hand and mouth wide open.

With *Heartbreak Hotel* having spent seven weeks at number one, Elvis was hot property. Further

nationally networked television appearances arranged by Parker had helped him build on his recording success – and he proved a natural performer. Before long he became one of the highest paid stars on television. The camera loved him.  His talent and voice combined with good looks, sex appeal and electrifying, energetic and unconfined performances brought him phenomenal fame and attention.

It is hard to overstate the impact Elvis Presley made on late 1950s America. He didn't just stand out because of his new sound, but also because he was so completely different to any of his predecessors in the way he performed on stage.

His trademark wiggling, quivering, shaking and pelvis-thrusting style earned him the nickname 'Elvis the Pelvis' and led to outrage and controversy as some journalists and older viewers considered his gyrating hips to be improper, even obscene. This led to him sometimes being filmed for television from the waist up. But in concert no such censoring was possible!

Elvis was central to the birth of rock and roll and the kids loved it – although their parents, used to the rather calmer, crooning performances of singers such as Bing Crosby and Frank Sinatra, were appalled. While he was incredibly popular with his teenage fanbase, he was not a hit with older audiences and religious groups. But if anything, their disdain for him just fuelled his new-found celebrity.

Elvis's other major hit single in 1956 was the double A-side *Don't Be Cruel /Hound Dog* which between them topped the American pop charts for 11 weeks – a record that stood for 36 years – while also simultaneously making number one on the US country and R&B charts. By 1958 the single had become only the third song in history to sell more than three million copies, after Bing Crosby's *White*

Reindeer. It is Elvis' best- selling song of all.

*Hound Dog*, written by the songwriting team of Jerry Leiber and Mike Stoller, had the most initial success and was promoted with another performance on *The Milton Berle Show*. This Elvis appearance is considered one of his most controversially sensual and attracted complaints galore. Consequently, when Elvis appeared a few weeks later, on *The Steve Allen Show,* the host said he hoped Elvis would give a performance 'that the whole family can watch and enjoy'. By this he meant that he was orchestrating a pared-back delivery of the song which commentators felt humiliated Elvis who, dressed in a coat- tailed suit, was made to sing his song very literally to a Bassett Hound which was dressed up in a top hat and bow tie. Elvis later

said it was the most ridiculous performance of his career. But he went along with it purely so as not to tarnish his image. By now he was being described as everything from 'lewd and vulgar', to 'obscene and morally degenerate' by his detractors.

Certainly, the sexual component of his movements was earth-shattering for teenagers who, for the first time, had something to claim as their own. His style had come naturally to him, and although he could not have known for sure how it would resonate with young people, it certainly did.

Within months he had risen to unimaginable heights of fame and popularity - was there ever a 21-year-old with such power and appeal?

*Performing on stage circa 1956*

LEFT _____

Elvis Presley and Johnny Cash pose for a portrait in December of 1957 in Memphis, Tennessee

ABOVE _____

Presley portrait in 1956 in Memphis, Tennessee

RIGHT _____

Various memorabilia from 1956 & 57

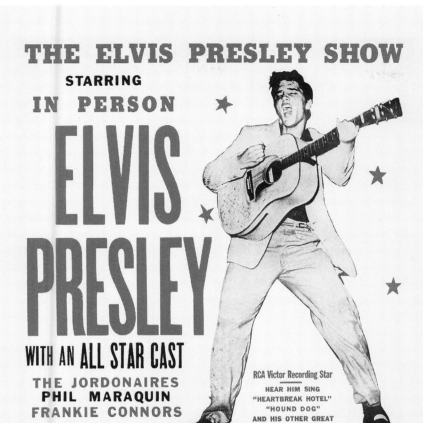

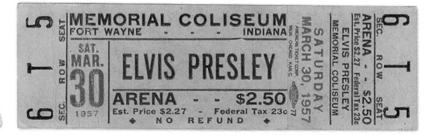

16

1956

# Making it Big

1958

With Elvis's profile and fame now rocketing, Parker seized the moment. He was all about finding new ways to monetise his protegee. Elvis once said that he didn't think he would ever have 'been very big if it wasn't for him [Parker]. He's a very smart man'.

Firstly, Parker signed a $40,000 merchandising deal which brought in $22 million by the end of 1956 through the sale of anything and everything 'Elvis-branded' - from hats and handkerchiefs to record players and even stuffed toy hound dogs. There was seemingly no limit to his inventiveness. It's said he even sold 'I Hate Elvis' badges as well so as not to miss the chance to make some money from people who weren't buying the records.

Parker was breaking new ground in celebrity merchandising - though of course he had a vested interest as, like any manager, he took a share of profits with some 25 per cent of Elvis's earnings from all income streams coming his way.

However, in April 1956, Parker made a rare misjudgement by booking Elvis into Las Vegas where the audiences were generally too old to be existing fans or won over by the set. Sensing the mood after a couple of shows, Parker cut the engagement from a planned month to a fortnight. Even so it was a long time for Elvis to suffer the chilly reception he received there and for years afterwards Elvis would remember those weeks as amongst the worst of his career.

But generally, Parker was a quite brilliant manager. Having exploited the power of television when others didn't see it or would have shunned the opportunity for fear of over exposure, he decided Elvis needed an even bigger screen – a movie screen. When Elvis had first talked with Parker about his future he had expressed his hope to work as an actor one day. He certainly had some ability, evident from his very early television show appearances where he would perform well during little skits and comedy interludes with his hosts.

So, Parker's second master stroke was to arrange for Elvis to screen test with Paramount Pictures – one of the biggest studios in the country. Elvis lip-synced to his hit *Blue Suede Shoes* and performed scenes from a film called *The Rainmaker*.

The Paramount bosses liked what they saw and offered Elvis a seven-picture deal. Parker came along as part of the deal of course, sorting himself out with an office and staff at the studios.

The speed at which life was changing for Elvis was truly giddying. It was hard to take in at first and didn't seem as if it would last; 'I might be herding sheep next year', Elvis would tell reporters, only half joking. But it was difficult not to be seduced by the trappings of success such as new cars and even a new house for his parents. His father Vernon was evidently happy at his son's extraordinary change in fortunes. Only Gladys sounded a note of caution. Frightened by the hysteria that her son engendered in his female fans she would warn Elvis that Parker 'is going to work you to your death'.

Already Elvis was becoming the 'property' of Parker, the money men and the fans. He wasn't really in charge of his own life or able to move around freely, and if he did try to strike out with an idea of his own he would often be reprimanded by Parker. Songwriter Mike Stoller – of partnership Leiber and Stoller who wrote many hits for Elvis – observed that Parker and his entourage kept Elvis 'separate ... he was removed', under the guise of protecting him.

But it all happened by degree and Elvis was so busy working that it wasn't apparent to him at the time. He had never been afraid of hard work and during 1956 undertook 191 concerts in between his acting and recording commitments. The money kept rolling in and the fan numbers kept rising. Although Gladys and Vernon didn't particularly mind the girls hanging around

*Elvis Presley promoting the movie Love me tender directed by Robert D. Webb*

the new $40,000 four-bedroom, ranch-style house Elvis had bought them at 1034 Audubon Drive, Memphis, and would be very hospitable, the neighbours were not so happy. The property simply wasn't private enough and fans blocked the street with their cars as they sat there with the music turned up loud or camped on the front lawns. Rumours about a petition requesting that the Presley family leave the street began to circulate and upset Gladys. It was time to move again and Vernon was given the job of finding a more private and secure place without any neighbours to upset.

Meanwhile Elvis would add another string to his entertaining bow. He wanted to be a serious actor, emulating stars of the time like James Dean, Tony Curtis and Marlon Brando. While Parker liked the idea of another income stream, he had other ideas about the type of roles Elvis should take, spotting an opportunity to use the films to cross-promote the music, and so persuaded Elvis to sing in his films.

This decision was seemingly vindicated when the single from Elvis's first film, *Love Me Tender* attracted advance orders of one million copies. It went on to sell two million and become the first instance of a single receiving a gold disc before it was released.

Elvis made his acting debut in November 1956, appearing as Clint Reno in the black and white western film *Love Me Tender* which was set at the end of the American civil war. Originally entitled 'The Reno Brothers' (who fall in love with the same girl) music was added to give Elvis a chance to sing and the title was changed to capitalise on the success of the pre-released single *Love Me Tender*, which Elvis sang on the popular *Ed Sullivan Show* during a break from filming.

After less than a year of mass media exposure, Elvis ended 1956 as a rock and roll global icon and one of the world's best paid stars.

He had reached an unprecedented level of success; no one else had conquered radio, TV and film

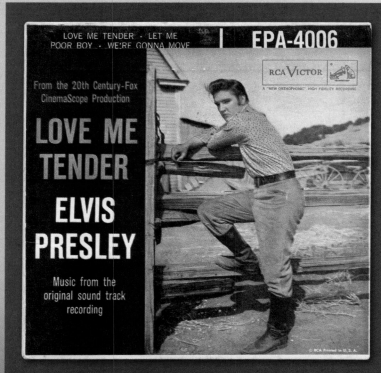

# Love Me Tender

Music was added to what was originally a straight acting role and the four numbers added to the film were released on an EP original soundtrack recording. This 'film plus soundtrack album' was a formula which would be repeated throughout Elvis's movie career.

## Track list

**Love Me Tender**

**Poor Boy**

**Let Me**

**We're Gonna Move**

**Love Me Tender (End Title Version)**

Elvis Presley promoting the movie Love me tender

so early in their career and there was simply no blueprint for how to navigate such territory.

How to follow that? Well firstly in 1957 came more hit singles, significantly the number one hits *Too Much* in January followed by *All Shook Up* in April.

*All Shook Up* was written by Otis Blackwell, although Elvis also has a writing credit for the song as sometimes happened in deals negotiated by Parker as a condition for Elvis recording the song.

Legend has it that Blackwell was inspired to write the song after Al Stanton, one of the owners of Shalimar Music, came into the company's offices shaking a bottle of Pepsi and suggesting the phrase 'All Shook Up' as a title.

Elvis is later quoted as saying he came up with the phrase himself after being shaken up by a dream he'd had and telling a friend about the feeling. With its laidback, shuffle rhythm and distinctive vocal

flourishes, the song went on to be Elvis' second biggest hit in the US, its eight-week run at the top of the US Billboard Hot 100 chart beginning on 13 April 1957.

*All Shook Up* also gave Elvis his first UK number one, staying at the top of the singles chart for seven weeks and introducing the British public to the 'Fuzzy tree' through its first verse: 'Well a bless my soul, what's a wrong with me? I'm itchin' like a man on a fuzzy tree'. The tree in question is a type frequently infested with caterpillars which cover it with webs capable of causing an itchy rash and making the tree look 'fuzzy'.

When the single was declared the Billboard Number One single of the year for 1957 it gave Elvis the distinction of being the only artist in history to have recorded the hit singles of two consecutive years; *Don't be Cruel* having been the best-selling single of 1956.

In the summer of 1957 *(Let Me Be) Your Teddy Bear* gave Elvis his third number one of the year. The song was from the soundtrack of his second movie, *Loving*

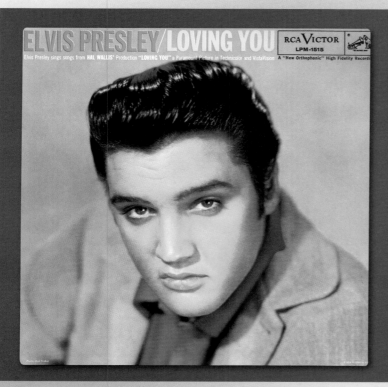

# Loving You

Released June 1957

## Track list

**Mean Woman Blues**
**(Let Me Be Your) Teddy Bear**
**Loving You**
**Got a Lot o' Livin to Do!**
**Lonesome Cowboy**
**Hot Dog**
**(Let's Have A) Party**
**Blueberry Hill**
**True Love**
**Don't Leave Me Now**
**Have I Told You Lately That I Love You?**
**I Need You So**
**Tell Me Why**

*Elvis Presley promoting the movie Loving You*
*written and directed by Hal Kanter*

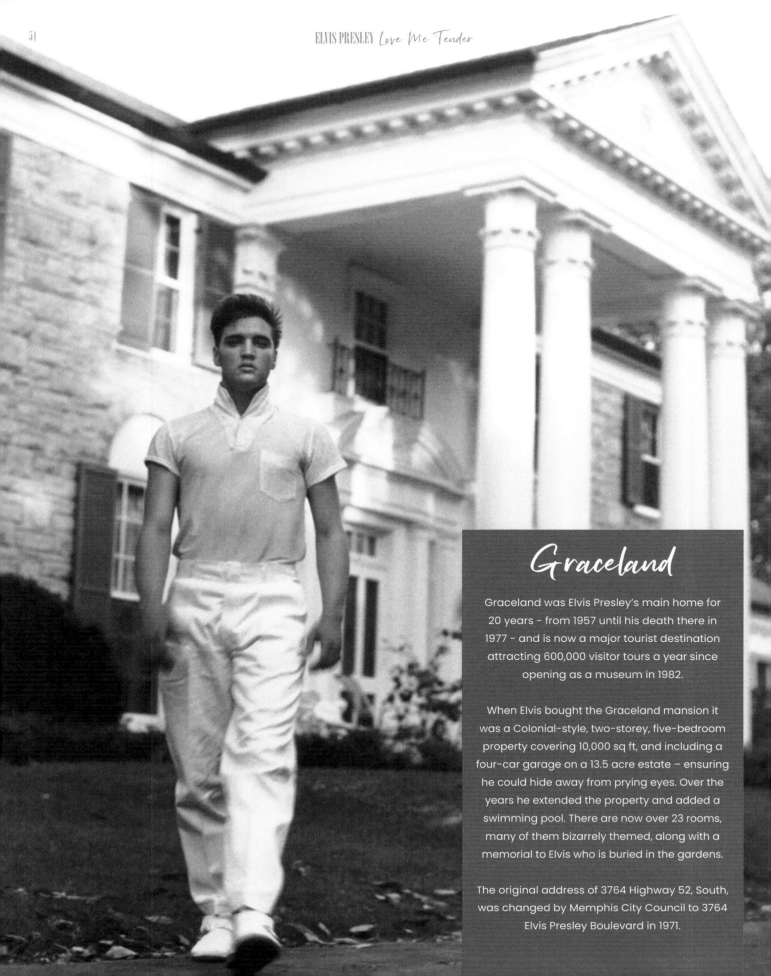

# Graceland

Graceland was Elvis Presley's main home for 20 years - from 1957 until his death there in 1977 - and is now a major tourist destination attracting 600,000 visitor tours a year since opening as a museum in 1982.

When Elvis bought the Graceland mansion it was a Colonial-style, two-storey, five-bedroom property covering 10,000 sq ft, and including a four-car garage on a 13.5 acre estate – ensuring he could hide away from prying eyes. Over the years he extended the property and added a swimming pool. There are now over 23 rooms, many of them bizarrely themed, along with a memorial to Elvis who is buried in the gardens.

The original address of 3764 Highway 52, South, was changed by Memphis City Council to 3764 Elvis Presley Boulevard in 1971.

*You* in which he took his first starring role, playing Deke Rivers, a deliveryman who is discovered by the manager of a band and propelled to stardom in an 'art imitating life' style. He gave a good performance, and the songs were mostly strong. It was his first full colour movie and triggered his decision to dye his hair jet black, which became his trademark look.

Fan clubs were now springing up all around the world, including The Official Elvis Presley Fan Club of Great Britain.

Now an established superstar, Elvis continued his gruelling schedule of concerts around the United States to huge acclaim and, of course, financial reward.

In the spring of 1957, Vernon found the Presley family a new home.  It was the house and grounds of Graceland in Memphis, Tennessee, which, at the age of just 22, Elvis was able to buy for just over $100,000. Although he would go on to own other properties, Elvis made Graceland his main home for the rest of his life.

That September, Elvis continued his string of hits with the release of *Jailhouse Rock* – the title track of his third movie which is widely considered the best musical he made. A classic rock and roll movie, it captured his on-screen charisma at its height and established his reputation as a leading man.

The successful songwriting partnership of Jerry Leiber and Mike Stoller was employed once again. The pair were asked to write the score and title song for a movie provisionally titled 'Ghost of a Chance' with Elvis playing a 'good guy' and budding singer who has been jailed for manslaughter after accidentally killing a man while defending a lady's honour.

They came up with *Jailhouse Rock* for the main number which Elvis, clad in stripes and denim, performs at his lip-snarling, knee-quivering best during an elaborate prison dance number which became one of the highlights of his movie career.

The song was so obviously set to be a stupendous hit

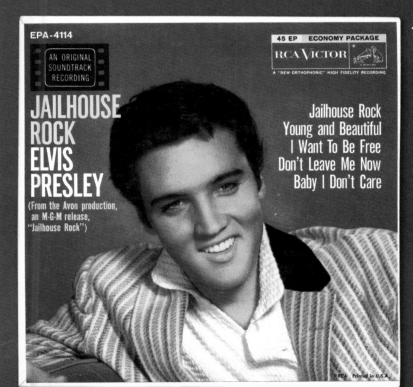

EPA-4114

AN ORIGINAL SOUNDTRACK RECORDING

45 EP   ECONOMY PACKAGE
RCA VICTOR
A "NEW ORTHOPHONIC" HIGH FIDELITY RECORDING

JAILHOUSE ROCK ELVIS PRESLEY
(From the Avon production, an M-G-M release, "Jailhouse Rock")

Jailhouse Rock
Young and Beautiful
I Want To Be Free
Don't Leave Me Now
Baby I Don't Care

© RCA  Printed in U.S.A.

## Jailhouse Rock

As with *Love Me Tender*, the songs from *Jailhouse Rock* were recorded on an EP. Released in October 1957, it stayed at number one on the EP chart for 28 weeks and was the best-selling EP of 1958.

### Track list
**Jailhouse Rock**

**Young and Beautiful**

**I Want to be Free**

**Don't Leave Me Now**

**(You're So Square) Baby I Don't Care**

that the title of the movie was changed to be the same.

The song includes an opening and repeating hook that is one of the most recognisable in music history – two guitar chords and two hits of a snare drum. It spent seven weeks at number one in the US and became the first Elvis single to enter the UK charts at number one, where it stayed for three weeks following its UK release in early 1958.

As well as that, the song reached number one in the US country and R&B charts and has gone on to be named among 'The Rock and Roll Hall of Fame's 500 Songs that Shaped Rock and Roll'.

Among the character's listed in the song's verses some were real people, although Shifty Henry was a musician not a criminal. The Purple Gang was a real mob and Sad Sack was a nickname used by the American military for 'a loser' during World War II.

Academics often cite the song for its famous reference to homosexuality behind bars - 'Number forty-seven said to number three, You're the cutest jailbird I ever did see, I sure would be delighted with your company, Come on and do the Jailhouse Rock with me' - which somehow bypassed the censors.

Its original B-side was *Treat Me Nice,* another song from the movie soundtrack.

The film was a success but while it was being made there were some difficult scenes in Elvis's real life. The bond between him and Scotty and Bill was not all that it had once been. While Elvis was undoubtedly the star turn of the old Blue Moon Boys trio, they were still a band together. Now Scotty and Bill inhabited a parallel, less glorified world in comparison, staying in separate hotels and of course, like The Jordanaires, earning a fraction of what he did. The whirling wind of fame was heartless

and about to blow them away.

Scotty and Bill's modest salaries were $200 a week when they were working and $100 a week when they were not. Having long been peeved that their money hadn't gone up as Elvis had become a star, they suggested to him that an instrumental album with him on piano might make them a few more dollars.

Elvis agreed to help his friends, but when Parker found out he had the project cancelled. Elvis was hugely embarrassed, but, as was becoming a pattern, didn't fight against his manager.

The incident was the last straw for Scotty and Bill who immediately resigned. Elvis called them to try to sort out the mess and persuaded them to work with him again in the future. But damage was done and it was a sad episode for the friendship which had launched Elvis's career and supported him so well in those early days.

Another problem for Elvis was that Gladys was becoming unwell. She had become extremely anxious and tearful, with her worries usually centred on her son, despite his career success. She feared he would be killed in an airplane accident, so much so that Elvis frequently travelled long distances by train. She also worried about the way he was treated by Parker, and she was very concerned that something would happen to him while serving in the military when his call up papers arrived. Underneath all of that she was quite lonely and missed Elvis being with her at home. She was putting on weight, generally slowing down, and there were dark puffy rings under her eyes.

But the huge money-making machine around Elvis meant that he had little time to deal with personal problems. He was needed in the studio to record another album. This was the *Elvis' Christmas Album,* which became his best-selling album of all time

# Elvis's Christmas Album

Released in October 1957, Elvis' Christmas Album remains the
world's best-selling Christmas album and one of the best-selling of all time.

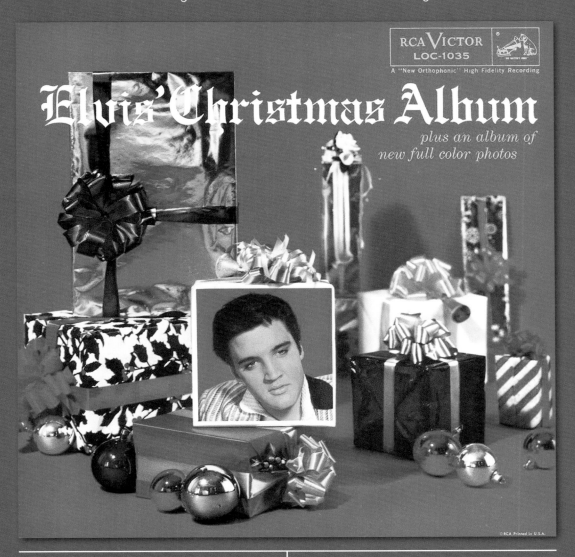

## Track list

Santa Claus Is Back in Town
White Christmas
Here comes Santa Claus
I'll Be Home for Christmas
 Blue Christmas
Santa Bring My Baby Back (To Me)
O Little Town of Bethlehem
Silent Night
(There'll Be) Peace In The Valley (For Me)
I Believe
Take My Hand, Precious Lord
It Is No Secret (What God Can Do)

This was something of a farewell gift to his fans. For, aged just 22, and having clocked up a total of 25 weeks at number one in 1957, there was a cloud on the horizon for Elvis. National service beckoned, which would take Elvis away from his fans and put his career at risk. Everyone wondered how his absence from the charts and his homeland would affect his popularity. Only Tom Parker viewed it as an opportunity to make his star act even more famous.

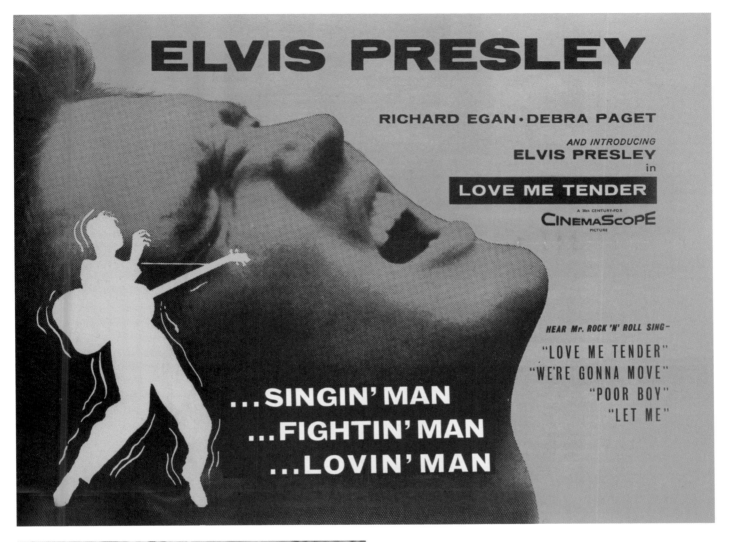

OPP. PAGE

Promotional shots from Jailhouse Rock, plus poster

ABOVE

A poster for Robert D. Webb's 1956 drama 'Love Me Tender' starring Elvis Presley

LEFT

Elvis Presley and Debra Paget on the set of Love Me Tender, directed by Robert D. Webb

Elvis Presley Recording in the Studio, 1956

Elvis Presley on the set of Loving You 1957

In the
Army Now

1958

All Elvis's performances on stage and screen were brought to an abrupt halt at the height of his fame on 24 March 1958 when, despite being one of the most famous entertainers in the country, he joined the US Army.

At that time America still operated a system of conscription, which meant that all healthy young men aged between 17 to 21 years old were obliged to serve in the country's armed services for 18 months. There were few exceptions and Elvis didn't want to duck his duty anyway.

Nor did Parker want him to use his celebrity status to escape any aspect of the draft. Although many people had expected Parker to be horrified at the thought of losing his star act to the US military, Parker was surprisingly sanguine about it. As ever he spotted a chance for even more publicity as Elvis transitioned from singer to soldier. He also thought a period of time in the military might calm Elvis down because, as his protegee was growing older, he had more to say about his future direction. Parker could do without input from Elvis, preferring to run the show alone. He would have a perfect opportunity to do that with Elvis out of the picture.

Canny as ever, Parker had kept back enough material and merchandise to release while Elvis was away. He did his best to reassure his boy that all would be well, as evidenced by the fact that within days of Elvis joining up, Parker had received over 5,000 letters from fans saying how much they missed him.

However, Parker did recognise the possibility of damage to the Elvis brand - it could be a case of 'out of sight, out of mind' so far as the fans were concerned. So he kept up a constant feed of news stories about Elvis while he was away. He made up many of them, including talk of future special appearances, but it didn't seem to matter. The important thing was to maintain an appetite for more Elvis music and movies.

It might also have been expected that Parker would join the Elvis entourage in West Germany. But of course, unbeknownst to anyone at the time, Parker leaving the US was never going to happen. Parker had to be content with ensuring Elvis was surrounded by enough company to keep him happy. He stayed in close touch by letter and telephone, all the while pulling the strings from almost 5,000 miles away.

When Elvis was first drafted into the services he was offered several special roles in recognition of his unusual status as soldier/superstar, including the chance simply to entertain the troops. But Elvis turned down all suggestions involving special treatment because he wanted to serve as a regular soldier in the army. This was often spun as being because Elvis was a patriot – which he was. However there is perhaps a more pragmatic explanation; as Parker said at the time, 'Taking any of these deals will make millions of Americans angry'. And Parker knew that would be bad for business. More importantly he saw a stint in the military as being good for business. Elvis still had work to do in winning over the older generations and overcoming the slew of negative headlines which swirled around him.

Parker was also conscious that as Elvis's teenage fans grew up they also wouldn't be so interested in his 'rebellious side' and so decided that his boy needed to gain more general appeal and become an all-round entertainer. He sensed that a few years in the army would be of value in helping to change the public's perception of Elvis, while at the same time providing a new opportunity to cash in.

So, apart from requesting a deferment to finish filming his latest movie, *King Creole*, Elvis and Parker asked for no other dispensations. Elvis even lost his trademark 'Pompadour-style' quiff when he sat in the barber's chair to have the regular short 'GI' haircut. At the time the US was not involved in any overseas conflicts and life for Elvis soon settled into a routine of sorts at Fort Hood in Texas where he completed his basic training. He was assigned to the

Third Armoured Division's 1st Medium Tank Battalion and let it be known that he 'enjoyed the rough and tumble' of the tank obstacle course. He also trained to be a pistol sharpshooter.

However, privately Elvis was less keen on army life and, feeling homesick and worried about the damage being done to his career, he fell into a period of low mood. Although he publicly eschewed any privileged treatment, he did get some special allowances including calls home and meetings with his girlfriend of the time, the model Anita Wood. Speaking to friends and family he was often tearful and worried that his fans would forget all about him. Writing to his friend Alan Fortas, Elvis said; 'I would give almost anything to be home.  You know it will be March of 1960 before I return to the States. Man, I hate to think about it.'

In June, during his permitted two weeks leave after having completed basic training, Elvis travelled to Nashville for a recording session at RCA. Several of the recordings from that session were released during 1958 and 1959 when, despite his absence from the scene, Elvis had hits with *Wear My Ring Around Your Neck / Doncha' Think It's Time; One Night / I Got Stung; (Now And Then There's A) Fool Such As I / I Need Your Love Tonight,* and *A Big Hunk O'Love / My Wish Came True.*

Back at Fort Hood, Elvis completed his training as an armour crewman in readiness for a posting to West Germany. But before he went, he faced one of the worst experiences of his life – the death of his mother.

## King Creole

Released in July 1958, this musical drama was based on the 1952 Harold Robbins novel 'A Stone for Danny Fisher'. In the usual fashion for an Elvis movie, the title was changed to match the name of one of the songs.

Elvis played Danny, a 19-year-old who gets mixed up with the mob and involved in a love triangle. The role was originally pencilled in for James Dean, but after the young star was killed in a car crash, Elvis was cast. He later said it was his favourite role and he took the job very seriously. Critics agreed his performance was impressive and generally praised it as being his best to date. The big hits from the successful soundtrack were *Hard Headed Woman*, and two tracks by Leiber and Stoller, the title track *King Creole*, and *Trouble*.

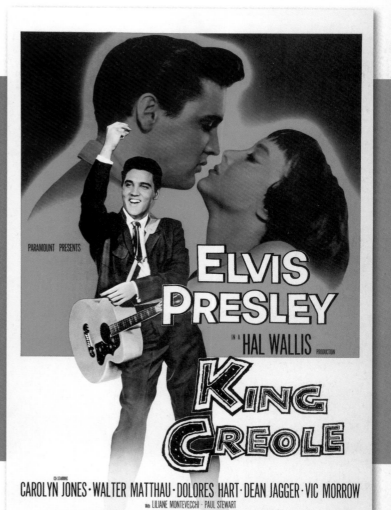

suffering from hepatitis and things were not looking good. Elvis was granted an emergency visit to her and had promised to return. However, he was woken up during the early hours of the following day, 14 August 1958, by a call from his father Vernon telling him that Gladys was dead, aged 46, from heart failure.

Several biographers believe that Elvis began using prescription drugs around this time, tranquilisers in particular, to help him sleep following the trauma he suffered seeing his mother in her coffin. He was so upset that others began to worry about him. The funeral director had to seal Glady's coffin with a glass cover to keep him away from her– he had been touching her and trying to hug her, saying 'Wake up mama. Wake up baby and talk to Elvis'.

Speaking later, Elvis explained that; 'Everyone loves their mother, but I was an only child…it wasn't just like losing a mother, it was like losing a friend, a companion, someone to talk to. I could wake her up at any hour of the night and if I was worried or troubled about something she'd get up and try to help me'.

Elvis had lost his biggest fan and fiercest protector and never again found that same unconditional love and closeness he craved.  Naturally, he was never short of female company, but he would never enjoy a lifelong love affair with a soul mate.

But Elvis had no time to recover from his huge loss. Within weeks he boarded the army troop ship USS General George M. Randall enroute to West Germany.

Keen to make the most of a publicity opportunity, Parker got special permission from the US Army so that he could arrange a press conference.  Elvis spoke to reporters at the Military Ocean Terminal in Brooklyn, answering questions about his music, his mother and his expectations of army life.  He posed for pictures and was filmed walking up the gang plank of the army ship – a task he completed eight times so that all the news outlets could get the pictures they wanted, carrying a huge duffle bag borrowed especially for the occasion.

As well as his army instruction, Elvis had also received orders from Parker - there were to be absolutely no performances of any kind, no entertaining the troops. And according to Parker's biographer Alanna Nash, his other piece of advice to Elvis was to be 'a good boy and do nothing to embarrass your country'.

Arriving in Bremerhaven, West Germany on 1 October 1958, Private Presley set to work. His duties were less than arduous, usually involving driving more senior officers around. He even had time to sign autographs for fans in his lunch hour.

Elvis spent a total of a year and a half in Germany, based in Friedberg near Frankfurt. Now away from the American press, he was permitted to live off base and he rented a large house in Bad Nauheim where he lived with his father Vernon, grandmother Minnie Mae - who was doing her best to fill the void left by Gladys - and best friends Red West and Lamar Fike, who both worked for him. These two formed the basis of what would become known as the Memphis Mafia, the group of friends and relatives who served and protected Elvis in later life. Elvis had been at school with Red and met Lamar during his Sun Studio days. Another friend, Charlie Hodge who Elvis had met in the army, was also a singer and he helped Elvis maintain and develop his vocal skills during his time away from the music business proper.

To all intents and purposes during his time in West Germany he remained in a 'Presley bubble' and was more or less free to do what he wanted when he was off duty.

This included having many women in his life. Although never faithful himself, Elvis demanded fidelity from his girlfriends and would be described by many of them as jealous and possessive. With

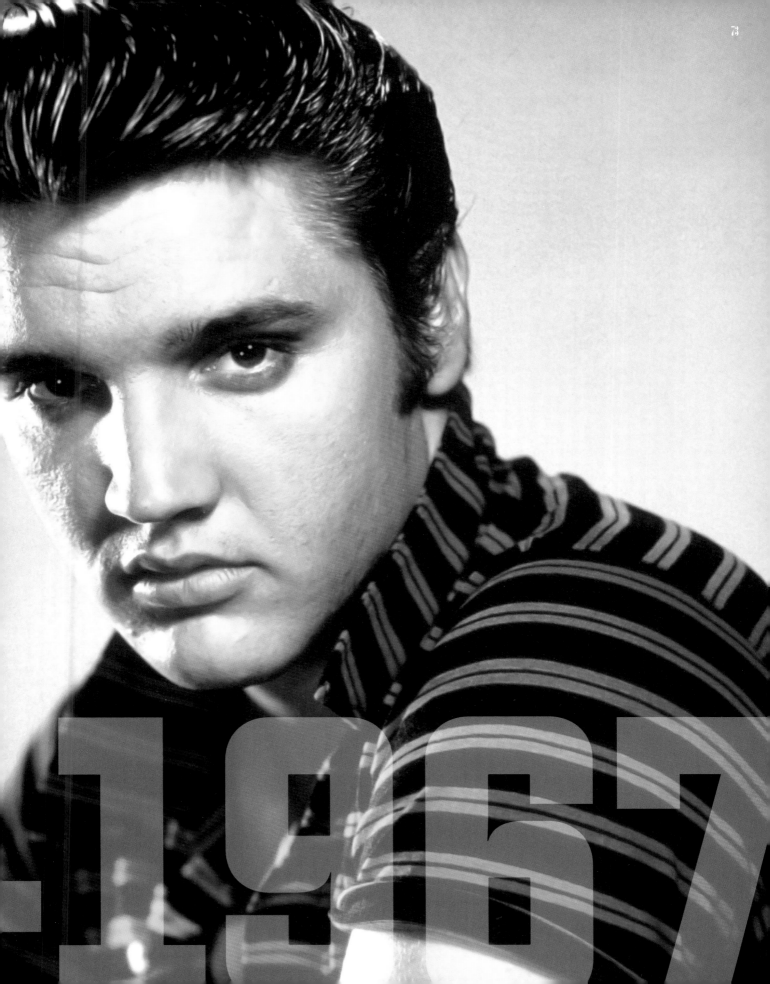

**E**lvis returned from the army like a conquering hero. Parker had packed his diary with work, beginning with a recording session which produced such evergreen hits as *Are You Lonesome Tonight,* and *It's Now or Never,* as well as tracks for his album *Elvis is Back!,* including *Such a Night.*

*It's Now or Never* went on to be a massive hit, selling five million copies in America and a million in the UK at the time and a few million more since. Making number one in most international charts, it was one of Elvis' most successful songs, and is still among the best-selling singles of all time.

Full of musical ambition, Elvis was on great form. His practice with Charlie in Germany was paying off and his voice had more depth, fullness and elasticity. His vocal range had increased and his control was more assured. He was technically a baritone, but with an impressive range of almost three octaves, could get close to bass in his lower register, as well as reaching higher tenor notes when needed.

Everyone was pleasantly surprised that he had lost none of his edge and was in fact an even better singer than before. He had also lost none of his ambition. He was keen to continue recording music, but also wanted to be taken seriously as an actor.

Despite Elvis being at the top of his game musically, Parker ploughed on with his own plans and deal-making, seemingly nonchalant about what Elvis really wanted to do. He was delighted to have set up a phenomenal deal for Elvis's first television appearance in three years.

It was to be on The Frank Sinatra television show, when Elvis would receive a fee of $125,000 to sing just two songs and a duet during a welcome home special. It hadn't taken Parker long to hitch his protegee back onto the wagon.
Sinatra had never been a fan of rock and roll, nor

was he keen on Elvis having previously said that his kind of music was 'deplorable ...a rancid smelling aphrodisiac...it fosters almost universally negative and destructive directions in young people'.

Yet Sinatra had evidently had a change of mind while Elvis had been away, perhaps keen to share in the young star's reflected glory, having seen the way the wind was blowing on the music scene. Sinatra's 'Welcome Home Elvis' show aired in May, helping to kickstart Parker's strategy of repositioning Elvis to make him acceptable to a more mature audience as a family entertainer. The show was a huge success, attracting a record breaking 65% of the viewing audience.

Elvis clocked up his 13th American number one with the release of his first post-army single *Stuck on You* in March 1960. The song also made the top 10 in ten other countries, including peaking at number three in the UK.

Then in April he went back into the studio to begin filming *GI Blues* – yet another boy meets girl vehicle to exploit his singing, rather than his acting talents. Elvis was disappointed in the plot and its soundtrack of uninspiring songs. Although he wasn't a writer himself, Elvis could spot a hit song immediately. He was sorry to have lost the talents of Leiber and Stoller, the incredibly successful song writers with whom he had enjoyed such success in the 1950s, after they fell out with Parker.

Singer and manager were at odds artistically, but Elvis never found the impetus to break away. It was hard to argue with the box office receipts, which again were huge, and in fact filming was so fast that it only took the usual few weeks out of Elvis's diary. It seemed that his time away had done nothing but boost his career and it was back to business as usual.

*Elvis poses for a portrait, circa 1960*

# Elvis Is Back!

Elvis's post army comeback album was Elvis Is Back!, released in April 1960, making number one in the UK and number two in the US. RCA were overjoyed with his outstanding performances on this album of 12 songs running to just 31.46 minutes.

## Track list

Make Me Know It

Fever

The Girl of My Best Friend

I Will Be Home Again

Dirty Dirty Feeling

Thrill of Your Love

Soldier Boy

Such a Night

It Feels So Right

Girl Next Door Went A-Walking

Like A Baby

Reconsider Baby

There was however one big change in his personal life when his father Vernon married again, less than a year after Glady's death. Elvis was not keen on his stepmother Dee, who Vernon had met during his time in Germany, and he certainly didn't want her usurping the position his mother had enjoyed at Graceland. He did however bond with her three sons, now his stepbrothers.

Not that he had much time to relax at home anyway. The films kept coming throughout the 1960s as Parker successfully turned Elvis into a soothingly anodyne symbol of wholesome youth. Where had the rebellious teenager gone? Any rebellion now was so gentle that he wouldn't frighten a maiden aunt, or more importantly to Parker, damage the money tree he had become.

And of course, Elvis couldn't really afford to rock the boat either. Despite his dismay that the movies were becoming more important than the music, both artistically and in income terms, he enjoyed the lifestyle they funded. With Graceland, its staff and another home in Bel Air to maintain, his movie deal worth $500,000 a film plus 35% of net profits was difficult to refuse. 'There are too many people that depend on me,' he said. So he kept his mouth shut, learned his scripts and worked hard. Later he also reflected that, 'I sure lost my musical direction in Hollywood. My songs were the same conveyer belt mass production, just like most of my movies were ... those movies sure got me into a rut'.

His old friend Scotty Moore could see what was happening. 'I just wish he could have got some real scripts later on. When they found out they could make some money off of him, I guess, well, he went ahead and did it – I will never understand why. He just wouldn't put his foot down on management and say, "I will not do this. Give me something." He did have a chance at *A Star is Born* – they had that in mind for him, and then Parker wouldn't let him do it.'

Rather than argue with Parker, it was presumably just easier for Elvis to play the game and keep the money rolling in. Elvis was now truly phenomenally successful. And his wealth and fame could distract him from any worries about the direction his career was taking. He lived in a bubble, surrounded by an entourage of favoured friends and family which the press would name The Memphis Mafia. No one earned much more than their living expenses, but had a great life on the back of Elvis, ensuring he was kept happy with jokes and unquestioning approval. Elvis was just 25 years old but lord of all he surveyed, unchallenged and powerful – apart from when Parker was around. Although Parker was the puppet master, the puppet himself had his own marionettes to boss around. Women were another way to pass the time – Elvis had a never-ending stream of casual relationships.

Scotty's opinion contained more sadness than criticism of his old friend when he said, 'With all the stuff that hit him at such an early age and so fast – he never really had a chance to grow up. He always had his so-called friends around him and he just never grew up'.

This 'arrested development' could explain why Elvis could contemplate a relationship with a much younger woman in the shape of Priscilla Beaulieu – the girl he had met in West Germany when she was just 14. The pair had kept in touch since Elvis had returned to the States and he was still very attracted to her, despite the fact she was still at school. Commentators have speculated that he had in some way found a replacement for Gladys in Priscilla and wanted to mold her in the image of his late mother. He would unburden himself to her during their long transatlantic phone calls and she would listen as Gladys had always done, becoming his special confidante and something of a lifeline when he was low.

He suggested to her parents that she visit him at his home in Bel Air, Los Angeles. Graceland seemed a less

*Elvis poses for a portrait for the release of his film 'It Happened At The World's Fair' September 1962. MGM Studios in Culver City, California*

attractive venue with stepmother Dee slowly taking over. 17-year-old Priscilla arrived in June 1962 for a two-week stay, Elvis having reassured her parents he would take good care of her. Despite these promises Priscilla spent every night in his bed, although she would always maintain she remained a virgin until their marriage four years later. Presumably Elvis also kept quiet to her parents the fact that he now swallowed amphetamines and sleeping tablets like sweets to help him get through life.

After Priscilla had returned to Germany Elvis embarked on a further charm offensive to her parents, eventually convincing them to allow her to move to Graceland. Her father brought her back over to America himself, believing that she would be watched over by Vernon and Dee and attend school. But in fact Elvis asked his father and his wife to move out. Priscilla loved Elvis but paid a price for moving in with him so young – she had no friends because she didn't actually attend school as promised and couldn't fraternise with other members of the entourage for fear of making Elvis jealous.

Publicly her existence was simply denied. No one said a word about her because everyone, from Parker down to the humblest employee, kept silent for fear of the bad publicity that public knowledge of her (under) age would bring. Their financial welfare depended on keeping quiet.

Elvis also kept secret from Priscilla that he had many other girlfriends. Although Anita Wood had left him when she found out he was still interested in Priscilla, there were many other women happy to take her place. One of his most serious relationships, almost causing Elvis to leave Priscilla, was his affair with Ann Margret, his co-star in *Viva Las Vegas* in 1964. But eventually that romance burned out, Ann Margret being too independent a woman for a long-term relationship between them to succeed. Elvis evidently preferred a more compliant woman, and during their time together he styled Priscilla

into his projection of an ideal woman. She looked almost doll-like in short skirts, heavy makeup and long eyelashes, with her hair dyed black like his. Yet despite having his 'custom-made' woman at home, Elvis was restless and not very happy.

He did not like the route his film career was taking. But he had a real problem now. Although many of his movies were critically panned, they continued to rake in the dollars. In 1964 he made $506,000 from music, but $1,508,000 from his movies. In fact, during the 1960s, his film earnings beat his music earnings every year. Parker wasn't prepared to give up his share of that cash pot and Elvis felt that he simply couldn't afford to turn his back on it either. He spent prolifically and paid huge taxes. Yet this habit of spending money with reckless abandon was at odds with Elvis's morbid fear of poverty. He and Vernon could well remember when they had nothing and desperately feared a return to such times. Elvis was also concerned about losing his fame, of not being recognized, not bathing in the glory from of the fans who constantly gathered outside the gates of Graceland. He couldn't risk losing everything, despite his personal feelings.

His 1964 film, *Viva Las Vegas* was a success, but then followed by four rather more dire productions. His singing career seemed to have gone to bed like he did in those days, loaded with sleeping pills. Would it ever spring back to life? Sales of the normally reliable movie soundtracks were slowing too, as the songs became more insipid. Because Parker had arranged the contract with RCA which tied Elvis to Hill and Range songs, Elvis could only record material from writers prepared to sign away their own rights. Some of the best in the business weren't prepared to strike that deal, not even to have Elvis sing their song. Yet Elvis was contractually unable to look elsewhere for good writers and better music and consequently missed out on many great songs over the years.

Filming and the odd recording session only took up about four months of the year and so Elvis had quite

a lot of free time which he would spend watching other movies, going to parties and reading the Bible, despite the contradictions it would have highlighted in his own behaviour. He was convinced his voice was a gift from God and wondered if he was using it as God would want. In his search for enlightenment and further spiritual growth, Elvis moved on to look at some of the other New Age religions which were springing up in the Sixties.

By 1965 Elvis had gone two years without a top ten hit song. The rock and pop music he had inspired had overtaken him, leaving him apparently out of touch and out of date. Even RCA realised something had to be done before their star turn was buried under the weight and quality of work coming from British bands such as The Beatles and The Rolling Stones. So, in what turned out to be a great idea, they unearthed an old recording they had previously shelved. This was *Crying In The Chapel,* which confounding all expectations, made number one in the UK and number three in the US giving his musical career a welcome boost. He wouldn't have another top 10 hit until 1968.

The success of the single galvanised Elvis to produce another full album, which was not a soundtrack. He decided to produce a gospel album, with a big full sound, and including a church choir. He was very excited about the project. RCA were less keen on religious songs, which they felt wouldn't do well in the charts, but Elvis got his way and was vindicated when the album *How Great Thou Art,* was acclaimed. It went on to win the Grammy for Best Sacred Album of 1967.

Over the years the pressure to do the decent thing and marry Priscilla was growing. Parker was well aware of the morality clauses in the singer's contracts and the possible problems that such revelations about his private life would bring. Priscilla's father was also keen that his daughter was properly looked after. For her part, Priscilla was growing up, wiser about Elvis and his antics, and mystified that he still refused to consummate their relationship. He told her, 'I'm not saying we can't do other things. It's just the actual encounter. I want to save it.'

Something had to change and eventually, towards the end of 1966, Elvis proposed marriage. The ceremony was set for 1 May 1967, when Elvis was 32 and Priscilla a few weeks short of her 22nd birthday.

Parker and father Beaulieu were satisfied. Elvis and Priscilla looked happy for the cameras, although both must have realised the pressures they would still face. The adoring girls weren't going to disappear and Elvis seemed unlikely to let his marriage get in the way of his philandering.

Some 100 guests were invited to the wedding breakfast and afterwards the couple flew to Palm Springs, where Elvis had another house to help him escape from the claustrophobic atmosphere of Hollywood. Exactly nine months after the ceremony Priscilla gave birth to their daughter Lisa Marie, born 1 February 1968.

Elvis was now a family man and his life looked great from the outside. But behind the scenes Elvis was still professionally frustrated and consequently prone to periods of depression which he would try to alleviate with barbiturates, painkillers and sleeping pills which, taken together, produced a soporific euphoria. Something had to change ....

# Girls! Girls! Girls!
## Elvis and the women in his life

The lyric sung by his character Ross Carpenter in the 1962 film *Girls! Girls! Girls!* could equally apply to Elvis himself; 'I'm just a red-blooded boy and I can't stop thinking about girls'.

As a famously attractive man, Elvis could take his pick of girlfriends and had countless relationships. Many of his girlfriends have described him as a 'gentleman', although he was rarely faithful, including during his marriage to Priscilla.

Viewed through a contemporary lens, the fact that Priscilla was only 14 when she and Elvis began dating is rather shocking. However, in southern America at that time it was not so unusual. And Priscilla wrote in her autobiography *Elvis and Me*, that she remained a virgin until they married when she was 21.

Here are a few of the other women in Elvis's life.

His first serious relationship had been when he was a teenager in Memphis with a girl called **Dixie Locke** whom he had met through the church in 1953. The couple would hang out together at the movies and in jukebox cafes and maintained a relationship for some two years, while Elvis was touring and becoming famous.  It was only natural that they would drift apart during their long periods apart.

**June Juanico** was another of Elvis's early loves, and she was apparently highly approved of by Gladys. Elvis met June during one of his gigs in Mississippi in 1955. As before, the demands of Elvis's career brought their relationship to an end.

Then he often dated his co-stars, including **Natalie Wood, Debra Paget, Connie Stevens, Juliet Prowse,** and **Ann-Margret**.

After his marriage to Priscilla ended, Elvis spent many years with **Linda Thompson**, a former Miss Tennessee and became engaged to model and actress **Ginger Alden** who was with him when he died.

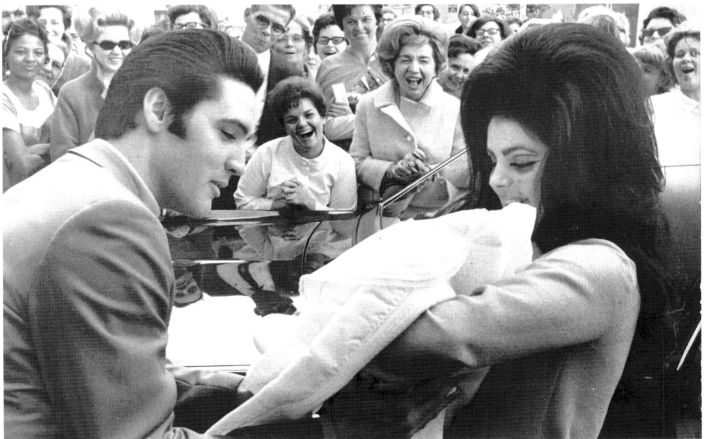

At the
Movies

Between 1960 and 1966, Elvis was among the top 10 most popular stars at the box office. No pop star since has cracked the movies like this. His films grossed an estimated $185 million at the box office in the United States and Canada – an average of about $6 million per film at the time.

**1956**
Love Me Tender

**1957**
Loving You | Jailhouse Rock

**1958**
King Creole

**1960**
GI Blues | Flaming Star

**1961**
Wild in the Country | Blue Hawaii

**1962**
Follow That Dream | Kid Galahad | Girls! Girls! Girls!

**1963**
It Happened at The World's Fair | Fun in Acapulco

**1964**
Kissin Cousins | Viva Las Vegas | Roustabout

**1965**
Girl Happy | Tickle Me | Harum Scarum

**1966**
Frankie and Johnny | Paradise Hawaiian Style | Spinout

**1967**
Easy Come, Easy Go | Double Trouble | Clambake

**1968**
Stay Away, Joe | Speedway | Live A Little, Love A Little

**1969**
Charro | The Trouble with Girls | Change of Habit

Elvis on the set of 'Girls Girls Girls'

There was no letup in filming for Elvis during the 1960s when Parker decided to take him off the road and make him a movie star. Beginning with *Flaming Star* in 1960 and ending with *Change of Habit* in 1969, Elvis made 26 films in the 60s, often as many as three in one year. Although he was one of the first and few music stars to make it on the big screen, this success came at the expense of his music career.

More than a dozen of the films were basically vehicles for a soundtrack album – many of which appear now in 'worst album' lists. However *Blue Hawaii* in 1961 is among the happy exceptions. Coming second only to the soundtrack of *West Side Story* as the most successful album of the 1960s, it includes *Can't Help Falling in Love*, which was to become an Elvis standard. *Blue Hawaii* was so successful that his management perhaps could not be blamed for assuming the public wanted more like that. The soundtrack sold more than 10 times as many copies in the United States than his comeback recording *Elvis is Back!* despite the album being far more critically acclaimed.

Elvis wanted more challenging acting assignments and the two movies after *GI Blues* - *Flaming Star* and *Wild in the Country* - had been serious attempts to develop his dramatic abilities. But they were comparative commercial failures compared to the fluffier *GI Blues* and *Blue Hawaii*. So, to an extent, the public got the films they deserved and seemed to enjoy, which were basically light musical comedies.

So after *Blue Hawaii* came a run of frothy rom coms. *Girls! Girls! Girls!* was also set in Hawaii - Elvis and Parker both liked the island and enjoyed spending time there – and received a Golden Globe nomination for Best Movie, losing out to *The Music Man*. This film included the big hit *Return to Sender* and gained Elvis a Laurel award for the best male performance in a musical for his role as an impoverished singing fisherman.

Another popular film was *Viva Las Vegas* in 1964. Elvis played Lucky Jackson, whose love interest was the actress Ann Margret. Chemistry crackled between the two of them on and off screen and they would go off together after filming was done.  Parker was reputedly furious. Firstly, he didn't want any bad publicity and secondly he didn't like the fact that, as he saw it, the film's director George Sidney was treating Ann Margret more favourably than Elvis, giving her better lighting and camera angles.  He did his best to ensure that any duets between the two of them ended up on the cutting room floor, along with Ann Margret's close ups.

By all accounts Elvis was seriously smitten and for the first time began to doubt the wisdom of his relationship with Priscilla. He and Ann Margret had plenty in common, including a love of motorcycles and would often take off on rides together. But after filming finished the affair petered out, although they remained friends. Ann Margret was not the person he needed to look after him and so Priscilla's position was safe.

Elvis continued to grind out movie after movie, seemingly regardless of their quality. People wondered whether he cared about what he was doing, when he knew the material was humdrum. The scripts became much alike, Elvis meets girl and sings songs. 'I cared so much I became physically ill,' Elvis said later. He was undoubtedly being stifled creatively at this time. Yet he didn't speak up. He wasn't good at expressing himself and tended to go along with what he was told was good for him.

Hal Wallis, an esteemed producer at the time, ran nine of the 27 pictures Elvis made in the 1960s, and said that, 'A Presley picture is the only sure thing in Hollywood'. And so things continued, despite the fact that while audiences came along, the critics remained unimpressed.

Then inevitably the quality of his movies diminished, along with the songs - there were just too many of them. It's been said Parker invented a version of MTV before MTV ...the movies promoted the music and vice versa.

*Elvis Presley in the film 'GI Blues'*

The 1967 film *Easy Come, Easy Go*, represented a new low – literally, as Elvis was cast as a Navy frogman balancing his deep-sea diving duties alongside a career as night club singer.  He finds some treasure in a sunken ship and sets about rescuing it from a rival with the help of a go-go dancing yoga expert.

The movie including the song *Yoga is as Yoga Does,* including lyrics such as, 'You tell me just how I can take this yoga serious, When all it ever gives to me is a pain in my posteriors'.

This is perhaps why the soundtrack sold only 30,000 making it the worst selling record that Elvis ever released with RCA.

Next in 1967 came his 24th film, *Double Trouble*, the tale of Elvis as a singer on tour in Europe pursued by two beautiful women, themselves being followed by some comedic jewel thieves and a mysterious killer.

1967 was the summer of love, including protests over civil rights and the US involvement in Vietnam, yet Elvis was filming a scene in *Double Trouble*, involving him singing the nursery rhyme *Old MacDonald*. His musical output simply didn't stack up against, for example, the huge *Sgt Pepper's Lonely Hearts Club Band* album from The Beatles that year.

Elvis was out of step with the times. He was simply not releasing any music to shake up the charts as he had in the late 1950s.

Compounding his frustration was a lack of concern from Parker. Yet still Elvis did not confront him. He had a lot of respect for his manager, despite being micromanaged by him.

Sandy Martindale, one of Elvis' girlfriends at that time, said in a documentary; 'I observed that the Colonel was in control. Elvis would stand to attention around him mumbling 'Yes sir'. He had no say so, no final approval of scripts. He could not say, "this is no good for me".'

By the late 1960s Elvis's career was in serious trouble. His increasingly formulaic and cheesy films made him seem quaint and completely out of kilter with popular American music of the time which had become increasingly linked to protest and the popular causes of feminism, civil rights and unrest around the Vietnam war. The Beatles, psychedelic rock and Memphis soul had taken over the charts and Elvis hadn't had a number one record since 1962 and not even a top 10 single since 1965.

The King was becoming a joke. Even RCA began to recognise that they were sucking the life from their Elvis franchise. Hal Wallis had also had enough, having tired of Parker's constant demands.

Elvis was on a slippery slope with both his film and his music careers drying up.  Something had to be done... and then the perfect opportunity presented itself.

*Elvis promoting the movie Kid Galahad. 1962*

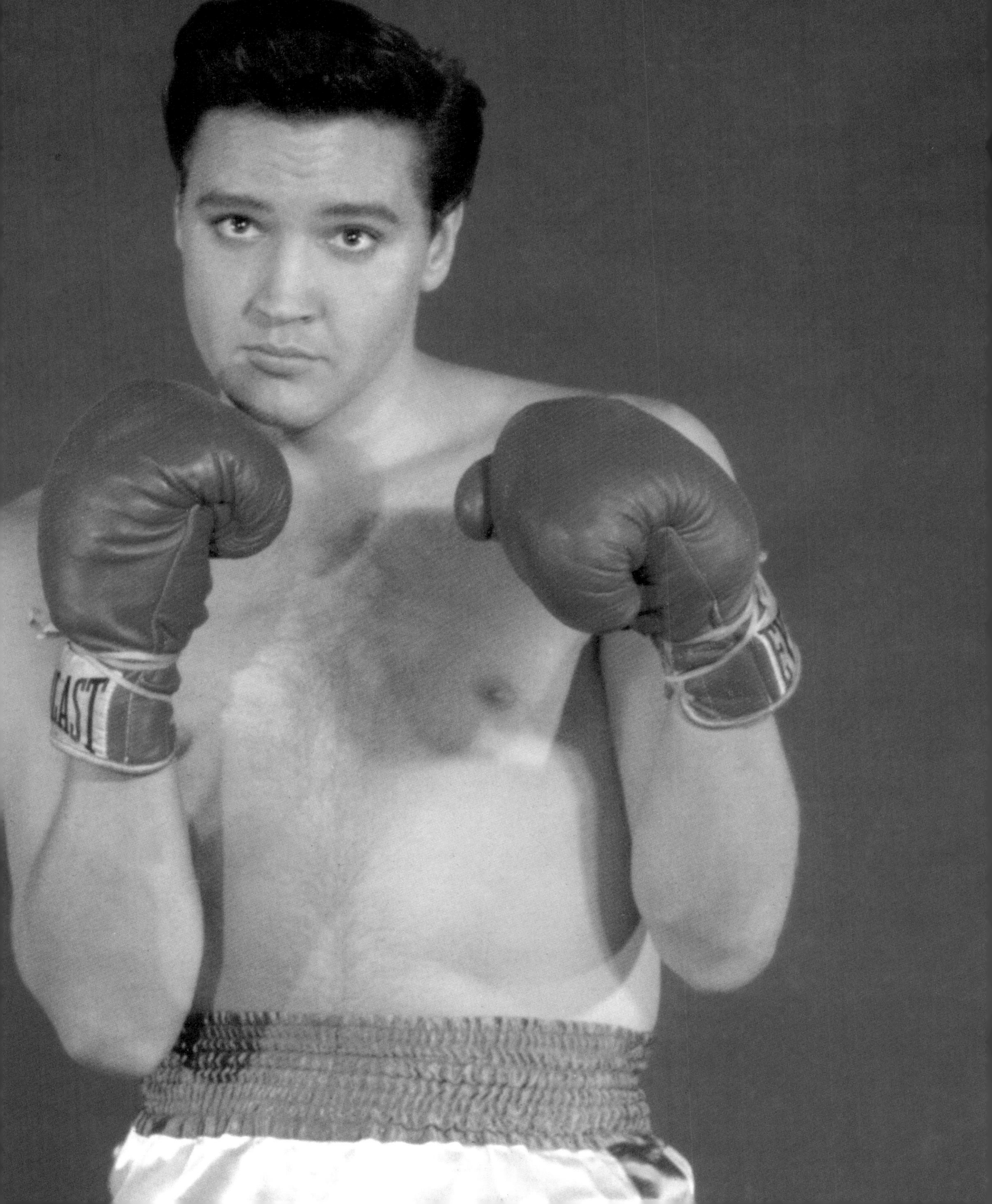
LAST

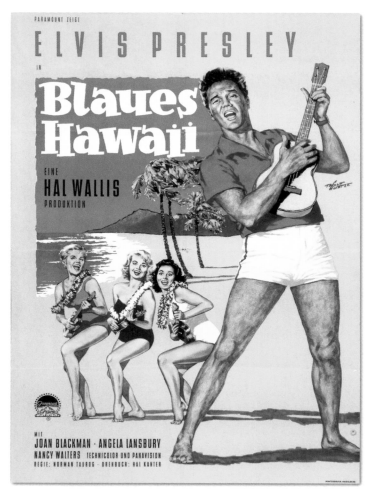

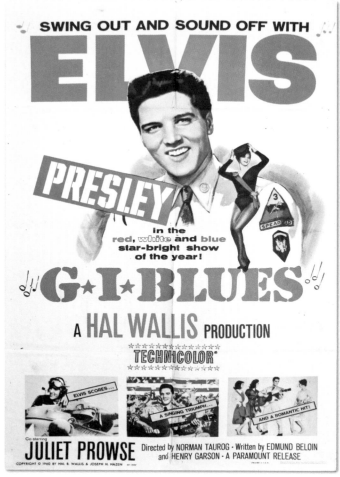

ABOVE AND LEFT _____

*Selection of movie posters*

RIGHT _____

*Elvis and actresses
promoting Girls! Girls!
Girls!*

FAR RIGHT _____

*Promo shot from G.I.
Blues with Juliet Prowse*

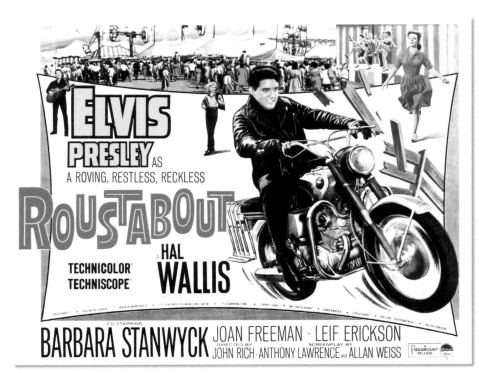

The
Comeback
Special

Cheesy as ever, Parker had set up a deal for Elvis to film a Christmas Special with NBC, the idea being that Elvis would sing festive songs that all the family would enjoy. Elvis could do that in his sleep. Instead, he seemed to wake up and stand up to Parker for the first time.

Experienced director Steve Binder was brought in to oversee the production. He had a good record in filming musical concerts but was not especially excited to work with Elvis initially.

However, he and Elvis hit it off and as plans progressed, Binder realised what a wasted opportunity it was to have Elvis simply sing 24 Christmas songs and wish everyone a happy holiday. He saw the impact the show might have if he could use the opportunity to take Elvis back to his roots. He and Elvis decided between themselves to ditch the cosy 'chestnuts round a fire-style' of programme intended, in favour of a more musically challenging, current, production with musical integrity. This was much more in tune with the times.

Steve had the idea of opening the programme with a stripped back, acoustic jam session. Elvis would banter with his original band, sing some original songs of all genres, from gospel and rock to ballads and blues, and reconnect with his old fans and his old self.

Parker very reluctantly agreed, if the show then returned to its Christmas format after the jam. Steve and Elvis then just went ahead and did their own thing. The tide had turned, mainly due to Elvis, who wanted the show to be a serious attempt at restoring his musical credibility.

And so it was that his 1968 TV special 'Singer presents… Elvis' - now better known as the '68 Comeback Special' - aired on 3 December and transformed his ailing career.

It was his first live performance in seven years and he was undoubtedly nervous - his hand can be seen shaking as he first reaches for the microphone.

But he had no need to worry – the show was a magnificent success, providing NBC with their biggest ratings of the year with 42 per cent of America tuning in. Viewers saw Elvis as himself; as for the first time in years he wasn't just parroting a script. He laughed at himself – 'look what my lip is doing' – and acknowledged his musical absence and the changes which had happened in the 1960s when he was basically trapped in a film studio. 'I'd like to talk a little bit about music…[he laughs] very little,' he said directly to the live studio audience.

'There's been a big change in the music field in the last 10 or 12 years. And I think everything has improved, the sounds have improved, and the musicians have improved, the engineers have certainly improved. I like a lot of the new groups, you know the Beatles and the beards and the whoever, but I really like a lot of the new music. But a lot of it is basically …our music is basically …rock and roll music is basically gospel, rhythm and blues and it sprang from that.'

The show spawned a soundtrack album which made the Top 10 and went platinum. Elvis had re-established his credentials – viewers saw him play an electric guitar for the first time – and reminded fans of just what they had been missing. His performance showed his old power and attack was still there. It was the reboot his career needed. The programme was recorded in late June

1968, during what was a tumultuous and tense summer in America, just weeks after the shocking assassinations of civil rights activist Martin Luther King and presidential candidate Robert F Kennedy, brother of JFK. Martin Luther King had been killed in Elvis's hometown of Memphis, Tennessee and so the tragic event had a special resonance with him.

Mindful of this, Steve Binder decided he needed a song to help show Elvis's reactions to the assassinations and bring hope and comfort to the audience at home during a very turbulent and tense time in America. So, at the last minute he had the song *If I Can Dream* written especially for Elvis to sing at the end of the show in place of the planned finale, *I'll Be Home for Christmas*.

The song, by Walter Earl Brown, was powerful, including the lyrics, 'If I can dream of a better land, Where all my brothers walk hand in hand, Tell me why, oh why, oh why can't my dream come true'.

Parker did not want him to record the song, but Elvis again overruled him with the simple words, 'We're doing it'. He then gave a heartfelt, emotional performance which moved everyone, and the song became hugely popular, making number 12 in the charts and going gold. In both the US and the UK, it was his biggest hit since 1966.

No one can know for sure what was going through Elvis's mind at this time and how he finally felt able to do something that he wanted for a change. He had been on his own spiritual journey for several years, flexed his muscles with the *How Great Thou Art* album in 1967, and now seemed to find himself again. Perhaps he finally understood that he was the most important person in the room, not Parker. As so often, his instinct proved to be correct. He, not Parker, rescued his career.

The 68 Special was one of the highlights of Elvis's post-Army career. Having been weirdly inaccessible to fans, other than via his stream of movies, for years, the 'King' had reclaimed his crown and reached out to his subjects live from Hollywood. The sad part is that he was never able to build on his new-found power.

Initially flushed with success, Elvis said he was finished with Hollywood, and he wanted to tour again. 'I never want to do another film I don't like,' he said, 'and I never want to sing another song I don't like, ever again.'

At first, he did seem to push against Parker more in an attempt to regain some control and be more relevant. But of course, he was contractually obliged to finish two more films, *Charro* and *The Trouble with Girls*. But the era of Elvis movies was ending; there would be just one more.

Musically revived, Elvis headed back to the recording studio in January 1969. He chose the American Sound Studio in Memphis, an inspired decision as it came with the talents of the soul sound of the house band The Memphis Boys and producer Chips Moman. Chips emphasized the rhythm section and brought in electric blues, country rural and gospel elements.

The recording sessions are regarded as another highlight of Elvis's post army work. They went fantastically well and included the song *In the Ghetto,* which provided him with another of his greatest hits, reaching reached number three in the US charts and number two in the UK and number one in West Germany, Ireland, Norway, Australia and New Zealand. The hit single *Suspicious Minds* was also a product of these sessions, reaching number one in November that year when it was released as a single – his final chart topper on the Billboard 100.

Critics praised Elvis's return to form, *Rolling Stone* magazine said it was unequivocally the equal of anything [he] has ever done, while Billboard said he had 'never sounded better and the choice of material is perfect.'

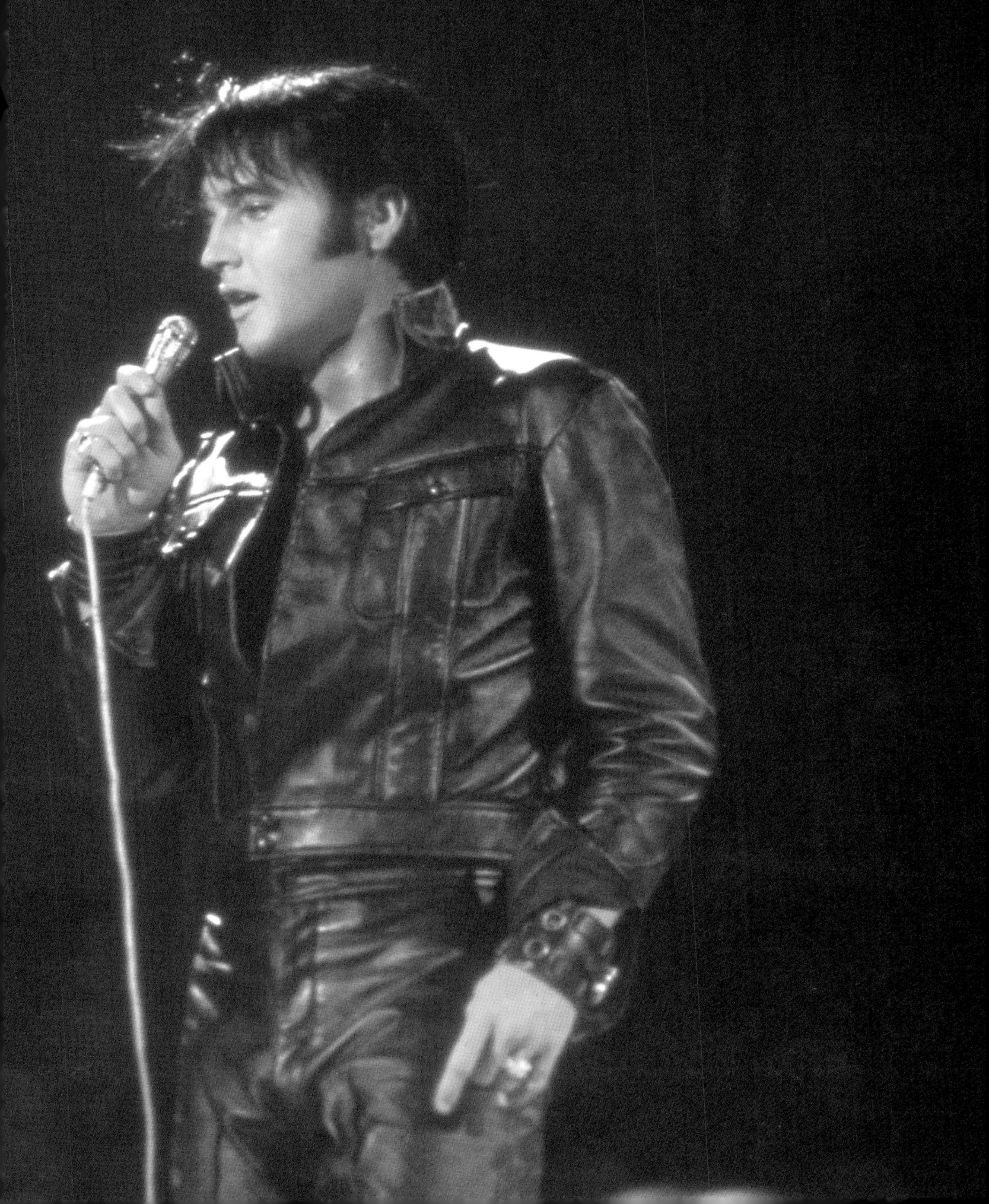

Now on a high, Elvis wanted to get hold of as many good songs as he could, telling everyone that he would go outside his and Parker's own publishing house if necessary. When Parker got wind of this he scathingly commented, 'Let him fall on his ass' and carried on with a plan of his own – negotiating a contract for Elvis to play a four-week engagement at the International Hotel in Las Vegas.

After finishing his final film, the forgettable *Change of Habit* in 1969, Elvis had hinted that he would undertake a world tour. Certainly, fans across the globe were clamouring for a chance to see him. But of course, unbeknownst to Elvis – or anybody at the time – that would not happen because Parker wouldn't leave the country, nor let Elvis go without him.

Instead, he worked his charm on Elvis once again,

persuading him to let the world come to him instead, by taking up a residency in Vegas. The deal was good - $100,000 a week for twice nightly performances six times a week with Mondays off. Elvis agreed to do it, though he did flex his newly found muscles a little over the choice of backing musicians for this musical marathon.

He would have liked Scotty and DJ and The Jordanaires, but they were already booked elsewhere. Eventually he assembled a group of musicians who would become known as the TCB Band and work with Elvis for years to come; James Burton, John Wilkinson, Jerry Scheff, Ronnie Tutt, Larry Muhoberac and Charlie Hodge.

The Imperials and Sweet Inspirations, a female soul group including Cissy Houston, mother of Whitney, provided further backing.

*Blue Moon Boys Scotty Moore and DJ Fontana were among the musicians joining Elvis on stage for the Comeback Special*

Opening night was 31 July 1969. The show was a hit and the 2,200 strong audience, studded with celebrities including his old mentor Sam Phillips, gave a standing ovation. Elvis said later that it had been one of the most exciting nights of his life. The reviews were great with critics unanimous in their verdict that Elvis was 'back' and firing on all cylinders.

Buoyed by this positive publicity, Parker began arranging a nationwide tour, and the hotel picked up its option to have Elvis perform for another five years every February and August for a fee of $1,000,000 a year.

The famous Elvis in Vegas years were about to begin ... rhinestones at the ready.

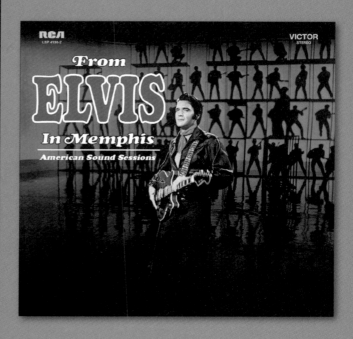

# Elvis In Memphis

This critically acclaimed 10th studio album was released in June 1969.

## Track list

Wearin' That Loved On Look

Only The Strong Survive

I'll Hold You in My Heart (Till I Can Hold You in My Arms)

Long Black Limousine

It Keeps Right on A-Hurtin

I'm Movin' On

Power of My Love

Gentle on My Mind

After Loving You

True Love Travels on a Gravel Road

Any Day Now

In the Ghetto

Caught
in a trap

1969:

A contact sheet of President Richard Nixon meeting with Elvis Presley
December 21, 1970 at the White House

Now he had to look after the symbols of his new office, so he spent money buying a police radio and a blue light for his car, handcuffs and, of course, guns befitting his status as a federal agent.

What was Parker making of all this?  The simple answer seems to be that he didn't much care what Elvis did, so long as he turned up and performed on schedule– much like one of his circus acts from the 1940s. Despite the fact that any manager should have a duty of care to his act, Parker seemed oblivious to the dangerous path Elvis appeared to be taking. Over the years various doctors attempted to wean Elvis off his prescription drugs with placebos, but he would generally find out what was going on and find a new doctor.  Commentators have speculated that in the days before celebrity rehab clinics such as Betty Ford opened, those around Elvis simply didn't know where to find discreet help and support.

Parker was now more powerful than ever, emboldened by the money he had made for himself and Elvis. Their relationship had morphed into a partnership as he now took an incredible 50 per cent of Elvis's earnings on certain transactions, with Parker controlling merchandising and other non-music related items. His justification was that he devoted himself entirely to Elvis, rather than take on other clients who would have brought in additional income of their own.   The story goes that in 1968, when asked if he took fifty percent of everything Elvis earned, Parker replied, 'No! That's not true at all. Elvis takes fifty percent of everything I earn.'

Having never been concerned that Elvis was largely unfulfilled by his life in the studio during the 1960s,

Parker now didn't appear to mind that Elvis was once again being ground down by his schedule and losing some quality to his velvety voice due to the vocal challenge of singing so much in the dry Nevada air.

 Like Elvis, Parker's personal fortunes had risen dramatically. His office walls were covered in pictures of him, dressed up to the nines, with his new celebrity circle of friends and influential acquaintances.  The former penniless immigrant was now moving among presidents and captains of industry.

Having always paid great attention to his appearance, he still liked to dress up – he certainly had the money to do it although most pictures show him wearing a big shirt loose over his trousers, his fleshy face framed by a cowboy hat.

Over the years he remained a controversial character, mercurial, with a temper. Despite his humble beginnings, he now had a fine opinion of himself and was prone to look down on others. Many of the people around Elvis would say that Parker barely acknowledged them and could often be downright rude and simply blank them. According to his biographer Alanna Nash, Parker had been bullied and beaten by his father back in Breda – perhaps this was his wrongly-directed revenge.

He was still a hustler at heart, with rigid business 'rules'. For example, as he wrote in a letter to Joseph Hazen, executive producer on many Elvis films; 'We do not mix our motion picture career in any way with a television career, especially if we are not in on the profits... This I learned from you a long time ago and I'm grateful for the teachings.'

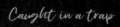

Tom Parker, circa 1970

He was of course an incredibly divisive character. But, having trusted him since the mid-1950s, Elvis was still minded to trust Parker and believe that his manager had his best interests at heart some two decades later.

Yet others disagree over the question of Parker's abilities. Famously the acerbic rock critic Dave Marsh described Parker as 'the most over-rated person in the history of showbusiness'.

There does seem little doubt that Parker's unwillingness to allow Elvis to tour overseas cost the singer millions of dollars, as well as denying him his wish and an opportunity to challenge and interest himself. Incredible amounts of cash were on the table to entice Elvis overseas, including a reported US$10million from Saudi billionaires, but Parker refused them all. In a 1982 interview on the Ted Cockle *Nightline* programme, Parker denied making any mistakes in his management of Elvis, saying of his critics; 'If they know so much, they should go into the management business'.

Parker had been married since the 1930s, but in typical fashion the circumstances of his relationship with his first wife Marie Francis Mott are unclear and according to Alanna Nash they may have had an informal 'carny' union. The couple generally lived a quiet and unpretentious life away from the razzamatazz of the world of showbusiness. Marie was very ill for the last years of her life with dementia, eventually dying in 1986. A few years later Parker married again, to Loanne Miller, his secretary since 1972.

According to Loanne, her husband never once wavered from his commitment to do the best job he could for Elvis. In an interview with the *Essential Elvis* magazine she said, 'So much has been written in a negative light about how the Colonel did this or did that to negatively impact Elvis in some way, and I can tell you that during the entire time I saw them together from 1969 until Elvis died in 1977 I never once saw a situation where the Colonel didn't do what was in the best interest of Elvis.

'There was never one time that Elvis was `forced or coerced' to do anything he didn't want to do. Every project that came along the Colonel made sure that Elvis approved of and signed off on it. You have to understand, the Colonel knew the business side and Elvis knew the creative side and they allowed each other to do their own thing. No one ever told Elvis what to do. Their relationship was very complex.'

Nash, other of Parker's biographers, and many Elvis fans, believe that Parker had a gambling habit and sent Elvis to Las Vegas partly to help pay towards debts he had accrued there. Certainly, he was seen playing in casinos for hours on end, betting large amounts of money. That might explain the fact that, despite having earned a reported $100 million plus during his career, Parker left only around $1 million when he died.

Things got worse for Elvis when Priscilla told him that she was leaving Graceland, taking Lisa Marie to Los Angeles, and wanted a divorce. His tame teenage mother-replacement had grown up. He couldn't change her mind, although the couple agreed to keep their separation quiet for as long as possible for the sake of their child.

While outwardly appearing to have everything professionally, Elvis had lost control of his family life and of his career, for a second time. He was in need of a boost. Then Parker had a brilliant idea and the whole team set off for Hawaii ....

*Backstage on the opening night of his comeback engagement at the Caesar's Palace Hotel in Las Vegas, 1970*

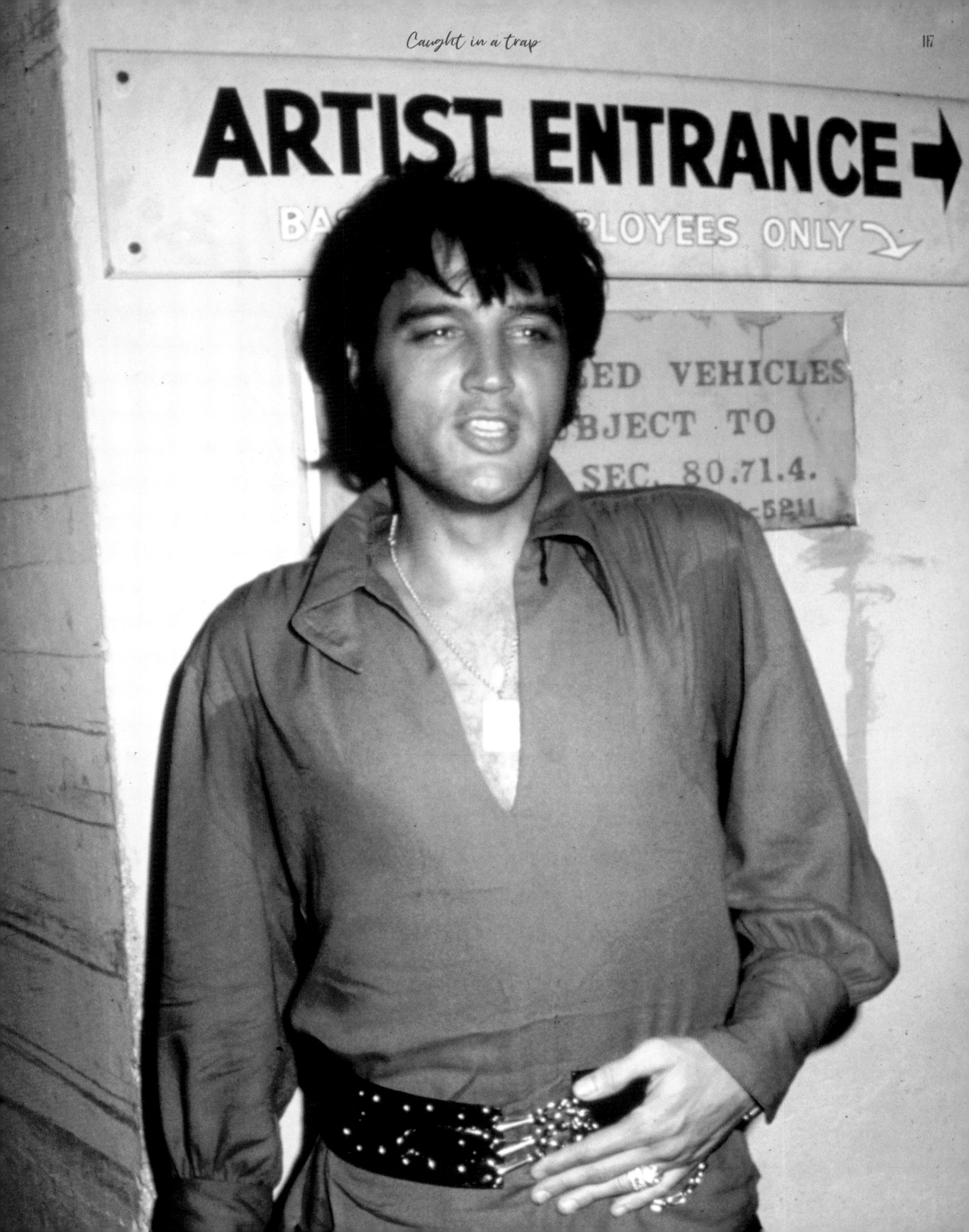

ARTIST ENTRANCE ➡

BA EMPLOYEES ONLY ⤵

ED VEHICLES
BJECT TO
SEC. 80.71.4.

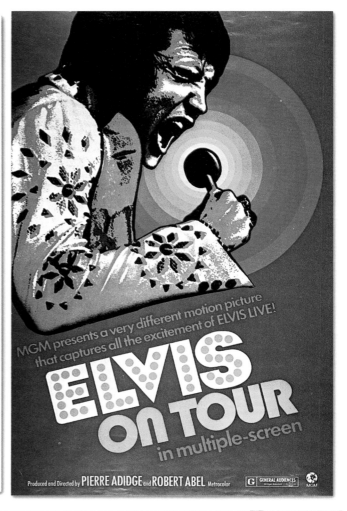

Metro-Goldwyn-Mayer présente ELVIS PRESLEY
**"THAT'S THE WAY IT IS"** réalisation DENIS SANDERS
PANAVISION® • METROCOLOR®

MGM presents a very different motion picture
that captures all the excitement of ELVIS LIVE!

**ELVIS ON TOUR** in multiple-screen

Produced and Directed by PIERRE ADIDGE and ROBERT ABEL   Metrocolor

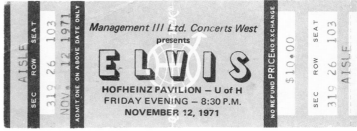

**AmericanAirlines**
In Flight…
Altitude: ①
Location:

Dear Mr. President.
First I would like to introduce myself. I am Elvis Presley and admire you and Have Great Respect for your office. I talked to Vice President Agnew in Palm Springs 3 weeks and expressed my concern for our country. The Drug Culture, The Hippie Elements, The SDS, Black Panthers, etc do not consider me as their enemy or as they call it the Establishment. I call it America and

**AmericanAirlines**
In Flight…
Altitude: ②
Location:

I Love it. Sir I can and will be of any service that I can to help the country out. I have no concern or Motives other than helping the country out. So I wish not to be given a title or an appointed position, I can and will do more good if I were made a Federal agent at Large, and I will help out by doing it my way through my communications with people of all ages. First and Foremost I am an entertainer but all I need is the Federal credentials. I am on this Plane with

**AmericanAirlines**
In Flight…
Altitude: ③
Location:

Sen. George Murphy and We have been discussing the problems that our Country is faced with. So I am Staying at the Washington hotel Room 505-506-507. I have 2 men who work with me by the name of Jerry Schilling and Sonny West. I am registered under the name of Jon Burrows. I will be here for as long as it takes to get the credentials of a Federal agent. I have done an in depth study of Drug abuse and Communist Brainwashing

**AmericanAirlines**
In Flight…
Altitude: 4
Location:

Techniques and I am right in the middle of the whole thing, where I can and will do the most good. I am Glad to help just so long as it is kept very Private. You can have your staff or whomever call me anytime today tonight or Tomorrow. I was nominated the coming year one of America's Ten Most outstanding young men. That will be in January 18 in my Home Town of Memphis Tenn. I am sending you the short autobiography about myself so you can better understand this

**AmericanAirlines**
In Flight…
Altitude: 5
Location:

~~approach~~ approach. I would love to meet you just to say hello if you're not to Busy.
Respectfully
Elvis Presley

P.S. I believe that you Sir were one of the Top Ten outstanding men of America also.
I have a personal gift for you also which I would like to present to you and you can accept it or I will keep it for you until you can take it.

EXECUTIVE
HE 5-1
GI 2/P

December 31, 1970

Dear Mr. Presley:

It was a pleasure to meet with you in my office recently, and I want you to know once again how much I appreciate your thoughtfulness in giving me the commemorative World War II Colt 45 pistol, encased in the handsome wooden chest. You were particularly kind to remember me with this impressive gift, as well as your family photographs, and I am delighted to have them for my collection of special mementos.

With my best wishes to you, Mrs. Presley, and to your daughter, Lisa, for a happy and peaceful 1971,

Sincerely,

RICHARD NIXON

Mr. Elvis Presley
Box 417
Madison, Tennessee 37115

RN/lf/cf/cf -                                                                gift

RECEIVED
JAN 5 1971
CENTRAL FILES

*Elvis wrote a five-page letter on American Airlines stationery requesting a meeting with President Nixon*

*Following their meeting in the White House, President Nixon wrote to Elvis thanking him for his gift of a Colt pistol*

*Elvis during a press conference after his first performance at the International Hotel in Las Vegas, Nevada on August 1, 1969*

ABOVE AND LEFT

Elvis holds a press conference on 4 September 1972 at the Las Vegas Hilton Hotel, announcing his upcoming concert Aloha from Hawaii

Aloha from Hawaii

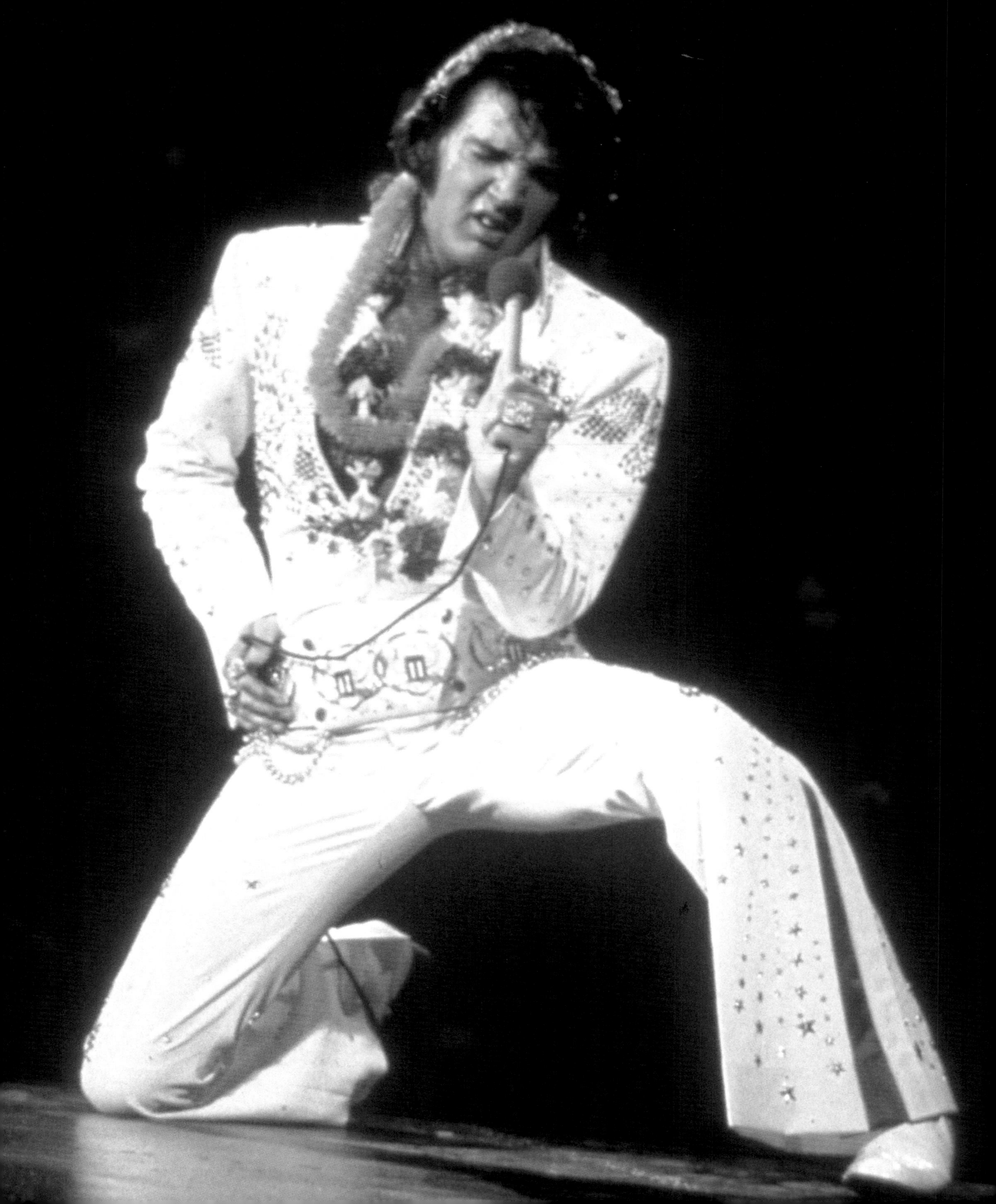

The next, and as things transpired, the last, big event for Elvis professionally was the 1973 Elvis: Aloha from Hawaii concert. Elvis was to make history as the first solo entertainer to perform a live concert broadcast all around the world by satellite. More than a billion people from more than 40 countries tuned in – Elvis, the king of rock and roll, was now undisputedly a truly worldwide phenomenon.

Parker reportedly got the idea for the broadcast after watching coverage of President Richard Nixon's trip to China. As Parker said at the time; 'It is impossible for us to play in every major city' so this was his alternative.

It was a first for any music event ever. RCA and NBC had teamed up to amass an audience of up to 1.5 billion viewers when the concert was broadcast on 14 January 1973, just a few days after Elvis celebrated his 38th birthday. He was reportedly terrified, although hugely flattered to be given the opportunity and got fired up for the performance.

His weight, which was increasing over the years, was usually a very touchy subject, yet this time when director Marty Pasetta advised him that he needed to lose weight Elvis agreed easily. Those in his entourage were surprised and delighted – none of them would ever dare broach the subject unless Elvis mentioned it first.

Elvis began another of his sporadic crash diets, this time restricting himself to just 500 calories a day for two weeks, so that he would look his best for the world. He also needed to do justice to his costume – an ornate white jumpsuit embroidered and studded with jewels of glass, complete with cape and emblazoned with an American eagle on the back. This outfit, more than any other, would fix the flamboyant '70s Elvis' image in the memories of audiences around the world.

Rehearsals had been filmed just in case of any hitches on the day, although all went to plan. The set list included many of his evergreen hits such as *Blue Suede Shoes, I'm so Lonesome I Could Cry, Hound Dog* and *Can't Help Falling in Love*. Its soundtrack album provided Elvis with his last chart-topper on the Billboard Hot 100.

Elvis had reached the pinnacle of his career with this show and everyone who was close to him was in Hawaii to watch. He had a new girlfriend, Linda Thompson, a former Memphis beauty queen, who he met in 1972 and had moved into Graceland fairly soon after Priscilla had left. She turned out to be another mother-figure for Elvis and as a southern Baptist was happy to read the bible with him. She turned a blind eye to Elvis's continuing flings and affairs with other women – he was never short of offers or opportunities.

Feeling the enormous pressure of the concert, he succumbed to a vitamin injection with amphetamines before he went on. This marked the start of another worrying period of his life.

Maybe if Parker had used the momentum of the Hawaii concert to kick off an ambitious world tour, Elvis would have been more challenged and interested in his work. Instead, after the thrill of Hawaii, he was back to the grindstone of Vegas and the International Hotel, which had become the Las Vegas Hilton.

It was around this time that Elvis and Parker had one of their worst fall outs. Elvis began ranting on stage about how the Hilton hotel's chairman, president and CEO had fired a favourite of his. Parker was furious with Elvis and went backstage to confront him. During a heated argument Elvis fired him. 'You can't fire me, I quit' retorted Parker who later demanded $2,000,000 to sever the contract. However, the spat was over in less than a fortnight. Vernon knew that they couldn't afford to buy Parker out, and so the hatchet was buried, and it was back to business as usual.

On another occasion Elvis lost his voice and had to abandon the stage. Then he missed three shows and had to drag himself through the remainder of his engagements. He only managed to keep going by using stimulants before the show and sedatives afterwards.

His anxieties were not eased when four over-enthusiastic fans leapt onto the stage during one of his midnight shows in February 1973. The men were tackled by security and also by Elvis himself, whose karate skills enabled him to dispense with one of the intruders. Feeling paranoid, Elvis thought that Priscilla's boyfriend Mike Stone had sent them to kill him and began raging to his astonished audience. Never before had he allowed his personal feelings to be heard in public. But now, probably becoming unstable because of his medication, he continued to rage for days afterwards and even tried to get a friend to shoot Mike Stone, who, as Elvis saw it, had stolen his wife and was now trying to ruin his life. Linda was terrified and in tears, doctors administered sedatives and fortunately the episode ended with Elvis saying he was content to 'just leave it for now'.

But the incident showed that he was now a slave to his prescription drugs. He knew them all and what they could do for him, the Valium, Seconal, Demerol and Nembutal amongst others, all of which compliant doctors could acquire for him. Linda, and everyone around him, was worried but nobody could stand up to his addiction.

Elvis overdosed on barbiturates twice in 1973, the first time left him in a coma for three days. As the year ended, and after his divorce from Priscilla was finalised in the October, he was hospitalised suffering from the effects of the Demerol addiction and a bleeding ulcer caused by cortisone.

Gone was the svelte singer seen at *Aloha from Hawaii*; now Elvis was described as 'having a gut' and on one occasion in Maryland he fell out of his limousine before slurring his way through a concert.

Had Elvis not been so wrapped up in his own world and suffering increasing drug problems, he might have been more concerned about the deal Parker struck with RCA who paid US$5.4 million for the rights to more than 650 recordings. It was an appalling deal for Elvis, who having waived the right to future royalties on those songs, got just one quarter of the fee after taxes - $1.3m - whereas Parker took half the money for himself. However, Elvis had reportedly needed money for his divorce settlement so was happy enough at the time.

'Happy' is a relative term of course. In fact, looking vacant and worn out, Elvis was on a downward spiral. The divorce was also depressing for him. Priscilla received $725,000 in cash, plus monthly payments of $6,000, adding up to $1,250,000, 50 per cent of the sale price of their house in Beverly Hills, plus five per cent of stock in Elvis's music publishing business. Additionally, Elvis paid $1,200 a month alimony for the next five years and $4,000 a month for Lisa Marie's child support.

After her parent's separation and divorce, Lisa Marie lived in California with Priscilla but made regular visits to Elvis. She enjoyed the best of everything during a lavish childhood, including ponies stabled at Graceland and private access to a nearby amusement park whenever she liked. It's reported that when she wanted to see snow for the first time, Elvis flew her to and from Idaho on his private jet so that she could play in the snow for 20 minutes.

His spending was out of control so that he couldn't afford to stop touring, even if he had found the will to do so.

*Elvis Presley in Honolulu
Hawaii. "Aloha from Hawaii
Via Satellite". January 14th
1973*

Elvis
has left the
building

1977

There was no let-up in the pace of Elvis's work schedule because tours filled the months ahead – he would give as many as 45 performances in a five- week period.  His existence was now fuelled by drugs, his performances notably lacking energy.  Unmotivated and overweight, he now sang for the dollars, for the young girls and for the fame - the music itself no longer seemed to interest him.

There were no studio recordings in 1974, although the concert recorded live on stage in Memphis was an album from which his version of *How Great Thou Art* would win Elvis his third and last competitive Grammy Award.

Elvis was now indulging in monotonously endless ramblings between songs, throwing out whatever came into his mind, from divorce to girlfriends, drugs to health issues, proving that his indignant anger at being described as strung out on drugs was a hypocritical façade.

The question remains as to how much Parker knew of Elvis's dependence on prescription drugs. Parker himself said that when he did broach the subject Elvis would tell him to stay out of his business.

It seemed that no one could temper Elvis's behaviour which was now out of control, along with his spending, as one seemed to feed the other.  Before the end of the year, he was back in a clinic for recuperation and, although he could catch up on sleep, he didn't get clean.

In 1975 he celebrated his 40th birthday, if celebrate is the right word with the press describing him as 'fat and 40'.

This milestone birthday brought on a mini midlife crisis - Elvis wasn't used to criticism, having generally received unconditional adoration from the day he was born. Now he began to wonder whether his fans would stay faithful to him as he entered middle age. Ignoring the planned celebrations at Graceland, Elvis spent his birthday behind the gold-painted door of his bedroom.

When his father Vernon suffered a heart attack on 5 February, he found himself in a hospital room next to Elvis who had been admitted after breathing problems.

This hospital stay should have been a further attempt to dry out but was thwarted by illicit deliveries from family, staff and friends. At least Elvis enjoyed a rare rest from work while he was in the hospital.

Nothing could ease his mind however and girlfriend Linda was worried by his erratic behaviour which included frustrated bouts of shooting in hotel rooms and expensive splurges on cars, planes, gifts and jewellery for friends.

His voice was seriously affected, the delicate top notes and the chocolate dark low tones had now gone. Recording had become a chore to be avoided and in February 1976 RCA resorted to bringing the studio to him. He did make the effort, descending from his bedroom in Graceland to record songs that had to be lowered in pitch to accommodate his restricted range.

The soaring tenor of his youth had been replaced by a faltering baritone. Among the songs recorded that day were *Girl of My Best Friend, Moody Blue, For the Heart* and *I'll Never Fall in Love Again.* Another recording from that day was *Hurt* which was described by one reviewer as an apocalyptic attack on the classic soul number and his most critically acclaimed song of the period.

But generally, Elvis's physical deterioration meant that he frequently had to stop singing during concerts to get his breath back. Often his backing singers would fill in the lyrics he had forgotten. Yet despite his continued health problems, there was no let-up in the number of concert dates throughout

1976 as Elvis performed in one tour after another. But the quality of his shows was now a long way from his peak years. Songs which were triumphs of his youth such as *Hound Dog*, were now relegated to be part of a seemingly perfunctory medley. The genuine feeling which had imbued *Love Me Tender* had given way to a shmaltzy rendition of *My Way*, the Frank Sinatra cover beloved by cabaret singers everywhere.

Over the year the phrase 'Elvis has left the building' had been fed to waiting fans to encourage them to go home. Now it seemed to be coming true, despite his physical presence, Elvis's spirit and enthusiasm had indeed left the building.

# Elvis Recorded Live on Stage in Memphis

## Track list

See See Rider

Medley: I Got a Woman/ Amen

Love Me

Trying to Get to You

Medley: Long Tall Sally/ Whole Lotta Shakin' Going On/

Mama Don't Dance/ Flip Flop and Fly

Jailhouse Rock

Hound Dog

Why Me Lord?

How Great Thou Art

Medley: Blueberry Hill/I can't stop loving you

Help Me

An American Trilogy

Let Me Be There

My Baby Left Me

Lawdy Miss Clawdy

Can't Help Falling in Love

Closing Vamp

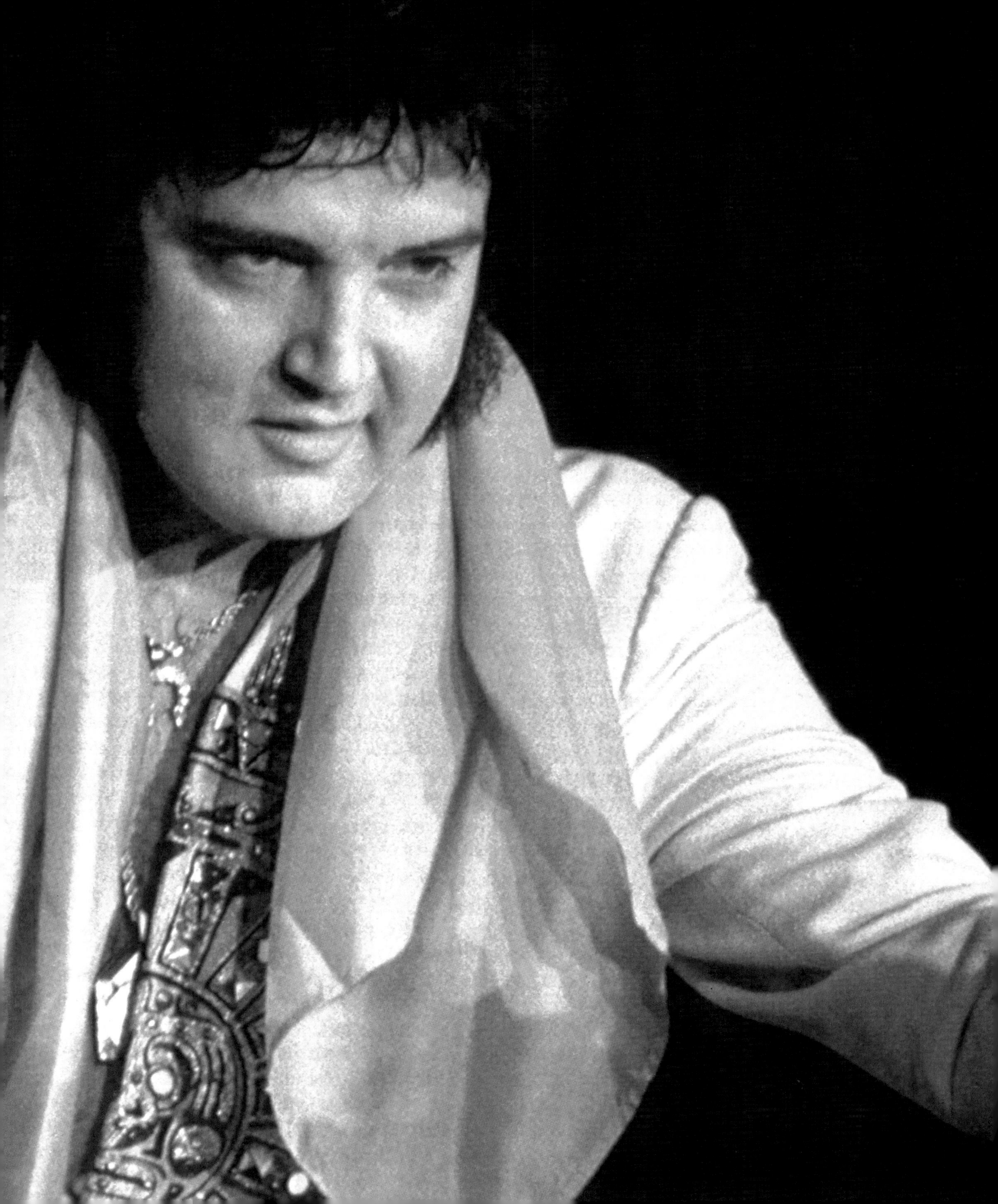

The King is Dead

By 1976 Linda had given up on Elvis. She was tired of wakeful nights checking on his breathing and hurt by his continued womanising. 'When you love someone, you don't want to think of them with another woman," she said afterwards. 'It all came to a point in my life where I just thought, I don't think this is the life that I want to sign on for'.

At the same time Elvis had found someone new himself – a girl called Ginger Alden, 20 years his junior, had taken his fancy and he moved her into Graceland.

But Elvis's delight with a new sexual victory was short-lived. Ginger wasn't content to join Elvis in his solitary lifestyle revolving around time in his bedroom reading books on spiritualism as Linda had done. Elvis did his best to keep her by his side, but she was not so obedient as his other partners and wanted to go out with her sisters and her friends. Elvis's reaction swung between frightening anger and pleading adoration. He would write notes in the night; 'I wish there was someone who I could trust to talk to' 'Help me Lord' and 'I feel so alone now'.

Old friends like Scotty Moore were powerless to help, having lost touch with him. 'The only time I saw him was when he was on video or something,' said Scotty later. 'The last time I saw him, I can't remember what the show was, where he gained so much weight and I could tell there was something wrong, but I didn't know what.'

Aged 41, Elvis returned to Las Vegas one last time in December 1976 for a two-week performance at the International. He was obese - his legendary eating binges, including his favourite peanut butter, banana and bacon sandwiches, having taken their toll - and using depressants to help him sleep when he was hyped up after a show and then stimulants to get him going again when he was still groggy the next day. His associates at the time said that he would regularly use amphetamines, barbiturates, narcotics, tranquilisers, sleeping tablets, laxatives and hormones.

Since 1969, Elvis had performed more than 640 stage shows during 15 engagements at the International/ Hilton Hotel in Las Vegas. His tough schedule which often saw him giving high energy performances seven days a week, two shows a day, would have floored an artist half his age.

Still he struggled on. His June 1977 tour was the last he would ever perform and has since become known as the Elvis Final Farewell.

On 21 June he gave a bad performance at the Rushmore Civic Centre in Rapid City when he appeared bloated and befuddled. His very last performance was 26 June 1977 at the Market Square Arena, Indianapolis in Indiana.

He then had a few weeks off before he was scheduled to pick up the tour in August. But Elvis died before that could happen. Although everyone knew he was in a bad way, his death was an incredible shock.

Ginger found him unconscious face down on the floor of his ensuite bathroom during the early afternoon of 16 August. It appeared that he had stood up from the toilet, stumbled and suffered a heart attack.

He was rushed to the Memphis Baptist Hospital in an ambulance, accompanied by his personal doctor George Nichopoulos. But all attempts to revive him failed and he was pronounced dead at 3.30pm. The official cause of death was 'cardiac arrhythmia due to undetermined heartbeat', although later reports stated that dangerously high levels of 10 different drugs were detected in his body.

Vernon was at Graceland waiting for news alongside Ginger and Elvis' nine-year-old daughter Lisa Marie, who had been visiting at the time.

Upon hearing of his son's death, Vernon stood on the steps of Graceland at 4pm and told the media that The King was dead.

The reaction from Elvis's devastated fans was extraordinary. People all over the world were grief stricken and in disbelief. Many came to Memphis to stand outside Graceland, most were weeping and inconsolable.

A few days later Vernon appeared on television, speaking from Graceland surrounded by enormous piles of letters from fans and beneath a framed portrait of Elvis.

He said: 'I would like to take the opportunity to thank you for all the cards and letters that you have sent since the passing away of my son, Elvis. We have all the flowers and the letters and the cards, which we will eventually get around to answering... the majority of them.'

Insisting that the fans would like to see Elvis back at Graceland one more time, Vernon arranged for his son's body to return there before the funeral. Elvis lay in his open coffin, dressed in a white suit, the mansion gates were opened, and fans had the chance to pay their respects to their 'King'. On the day of the funeral, 18 August, an estimated 80,000 fans jammed the street outside hoping for a view of the body; 30,000 were admitted to the house, leaving thousands more disappointed when the gates closed again three and a half hours later. It was a boiling hot day and many people passed out from the heat. In chaotic scenes, two people were killed when a drunk driver ploughed into the crowd.

After the funeral, a cortege of 16 white Cadillacs led a slow procession down Elvis Presley Boulevard to the Forest Hill cemetery, where the ground was covered with over 2,000 floral tributes including a hound dog and guitars. Elvis was laid to rest next to his beloved mother Gladys. Vernon said his final words to him; 'Daddy will be with you soon'.

Over the subsequent years, some fans have simply refused to believe that Elvis died that day. Theories include one that he faked his death to escape the media, and another that he had entered a witness protection programme after problems with his work as an undercover agent for the FBI. There were also reports of 'sightings' of him, particularly during the 1980s.

Such was his power and influence that some people just couldn't believe he had gone. The extraordinary facts of his life are simply that Elvis, born poor and with no connections, died in a mansion on a street named in his honour, as a cultural phenomenon, having changed the course of popular music for ever.

**...lle News**
SOUTH CAROLINA

...st 17, 1977    • • •

**...vis is dead at 42**

...Tenn. (AP) — Elvis ...Mississippi boy whose ...guitar and gyrating ...a new style in popu... ...ed Tuesday afternoon ...spital, police said. He

...he parlayed a $4 trip ...studio into a multi-... ...business, was taken ...ency room of Baptist ...ering from what hos-...said was respiratory

...C. Nichopoulos, ...sonal physician, said ...attack was a possible ...th, but that he could ...until after a post mor-...

...McLaughlin of the ...lice Department de-...er report that detec-...vestigating a possible

...ot investigating the ...said McLaughlin. "I ...here that information ...at it's not so." ...of people gathered at ...and at Presley's Gra-

Hospital officials said the enter-tainer was found unconscious at his home by his road manager, Joe Esposito.

Esposito began resuscitation ef-forts and called a fire department ambulance. Emergency medical technicians with the ambulance continued cardiopulmonary resus-citation efforts on the way to the hospital.

Nichopoulos halted resuscitation attempts at about 3:30 p.m. (4:30 p.m. EDT), according to the hospital

Presley had been a frequent pa-tient at the hospital over the past few years.

When he was rumored to be suf-fering from various incurable dis-eases, his physicians had blamed his hospitalizations on eye trouble, a twisted colon and on exhaustion.

Earlier this year, he cancelled several performances in Louisiana and returned to Memphis where he was hospitalized for what his phys-icians said was exhaustion.

He had rarely been seen in pub-lic recently, and his weight was

an 11-day tour to begin Wednesday in Portland, Maine.

Presley's gyrating hips were only mildly suggestive compared to most of today's rock performers. But when he appeared on the Ed Sullivan Show in the 1950's, fears his sexuality seemed so overt that he was shown only from the waist up.

"Everytime I move on televi-sion, they write that I'm obscene," Presley once said. "I've seen a lot worse movements than mine every night on TV. Look at all that mod-ern dancing. If I did those move-ments, they'd want to lynch me. Yet I never read anything criticiz-ing modern ballet."

His shake, rattle and roll show-manship – with such million sell-ers as "You Ain't Nothing But A Hound Dog," "Heartbreak Hotel," "Blue Suede Shoes" and "Love Me Tender," kept teen-age girls sigh-ing.

He performed with slicked back hair, sideburns and a perpetual sneer.

Presley went from driving a

---

# THE Sun

## HE WAS 42 AND ALONE

Wednesday, August 17, 1977      6p      TODAY'S TV PAGES 12 and 13

# KING ELVIS DEAD

**FAT AND FORTY** . . . One of the last pictures of rocking king Elvis Presley on stage in America  His overeating made him a tragic sight

## A massive heart attack at mansion

From ROSS WABY    in New York

**ELVIS PRESLEY**, the rock 'n' roll king who thrilled millions, died alone yester-day aged 42.

He was felled by a massive heart attack . . . and died in his mansion home before help could reach him.

Elvis, who had been ill for some time, was found by his road manager Joe Esposito.

Mr Esposito sent for an ambulance and tried to revive Elvis.

Then medical staff mas-saged the superstar's heart as the ambulance sped from his home in Memphis, Ten-nessee to the city's Baptist hospital.

### FATHER

Elvis's personal doctor, George Nichopoulos, who was in the ambulance, kept imploring the singer: "Come on, Presley, breathe. Breathe for me."

Doctors then battled for half an hour before announcing that he was dead.

Dr Nichopoulos said later that he suspected a heart attack was the cause of death, but this could not be confirmed until a post mor-tem examination.

Big crowds gathered out-side the hospital, where Elvis's 61-year-old father, Vernon, went with other

*The idol who had the whole world rocking*
Pages 4 and 5

relatives after death was confirmed.

"I don't know why we are here— we're just paying our condolences," said a middle-aged woman who stood with a throng at the hospital gates.

The sudden death will shock millions of Elvis fans world-wide.

But it was no surprise to those close to him.

For Elvis, the poor boy who became the world's highest paid performer, was the victim of his own phen-ominal success.

His millions enabled him to indulge his every whim, and that led to his undoing and his death.

His fondness for junk

food—hamburgers and soft drinks—became an addic-tion, as did his thirst for thrills and experiences . . . and drugs.

Elvis sought kicks with cars, motorcycles, women, parties, guns, pinball machines, pool tables and no timetable.

He liked to stay up late —all night if he was enjoy-ing himself—surrounded by the cousins and bodyguards that comprised his "Mem-phis Mafia."

### DRUGS

To keep his body going as he sated himself, he turned more and more to drugs.

Red West, a bodyguard, said recently: "He takes pills to go to sleep, he takes pills to get up, he takes pills to go to the lavatory, and he takes pills to stop him from going."

West, sacked last year, after a row with his boss and boyhood friend, re-vealed the extent of Elvis's drug taking.

"He was a walking pharmaceutical shop. He ...
Continued on Page Two

## DUCHESS BIDS TO HALT TV SERIES—Page 2

---

**...AL APPEAL** FINAL

August 17, 1977

**...f Rock And Roll ...After Heart Attack**

There's no way to be more ...that," Francisco said.

...Nichopoulos, Presley's per-...said last night he was not ...thing he did unusual yester-...y" and said "his fiancee ..." was the last person to see ...re his body was found about ...2:30 p.m.

...Presley's death spread, tele-...ope calls began pouring into ...m mourners and newsmen ...e world wishing to either ex-...ences to Presley's survivors ...lodging to attend the funeral, ...stations began playing Elvis ...cord stores in Memphis and

other parts of the country reported a run on Elvis records.

Memphis Mayor Wyeth Chandler said flags on all city buildings would be flown at half staff until the funeral.

Police said they were told Presley had played racketball at his home early Tues-day and quit about 8 a.m. when he told friends he was going to read.

Martin Davis of Chattanooga, a con-struction projects engineer with K-Mart Discount Stores, said he was driving south on Elvis Presley Boulevard when an ambu-lance almost hit him as it turned into the driveway at Graceland.

"The ambulance damn near ran over me," he said "It hit the gate as it was
(Continued on Page 12)

arrived shortly after 2:30 p.m.

A Memphis Fire Department ambulance from Engine House 29 at 2147 Elvis Pres-ley Boulevard responded to the call at 2:33 p.m. and by 2:56 p.m. had taken Presley to the emergency room at Baptist Hospital in Midtown from his Whitehaven home seven miles away.

**Hearse Takes Body Of Elvis Presley From Baptist Hospital**
By Fred Griffith

**... You Sure There's No Mistake?' ...The Desired Answer Never Came**

By TERRY KEETER
...OTIS L. SANFORD

...crowd of about 150 persons ...he emergency room entrance ...spital minutes after news of

announcement that earlier reports had been wrong.

"Are you sure?" asked Winston Meek, 63, of 1875 Mignon. "Have you confirmed it for sure! There's no mistake?"

tled other emergency cases into the hospi-tal area and kept the drive clear for ambu-lances. Hospital security guards and main-tenance employes kept spectators and the press out of the emergency room and the

---

# Dead at 42

Long live
the King

1977-

TODAY

The world had lost one of its biggest stars. But since his death Elvis has maintained his popularity; his music still sells, Graceland - his home-turned-museum- gets thousands of visitors a year and Elvis impersonators make a great living.

He remains among the highest-earning dead celebrities. In 2020, more than 40 years after his death, Forbes listed Elvis as the fifth highest earning dead celebrity with takings of $23 million a year. Graceland typically accounts for more than $10 million of his posthumous annual earnings.

Internationally, Elvis has sold well over one billion records, more than any other artist. His American sales have earned him gold, platinum or multi-platinum awards for 140 different albums and singles. Elvis's last record, '*Way Down*,' made the top 20 in the United States and number one in the UK charts during the weeks following his death.

Over the decades 'The King's' career has been kept alive by a string of reissues and deep vault dives, including a specialty label FTD (Follow That Dream) that issues several projects each year for his still die-hard fan base chronicling Elvis' raw studio takes, out of print soundtrack albums, and previously unheard live concerts.

Fans have also been able to attend concerts where film and archive recordings of Elvis's voice are played over a live performance by the Royal Philharmonic Concert Orchestra. Elvis gets a standing ovation 40-plus years after his death.  Long live the King.

## Vernon Presley

In his will Elvis had named his father Vernon, his grandmother Minnie Mae, and his daughter Lisa Marie as beneficiaries. Vernon was also an executor and trustee, a role he fulfilled until his death on 26 June 1979 aged 63. His mother Minnie Mae died on 8 May 1980 aged 89 and is buried in the meditation garden at Graceland alongside Vernon, daughter-in-law Gladys and grandson Elvis.  Gladys and Elvis were moved from their original burial site at Forest Hills Cemetery to Graceland on 2 October 1977, to give them a safer and more protected environment. Also in the meditation garden is a memorial to Elvis's twin brother Jesse.

## Priscilla Presley

After Vernon's death, his will named three co-executors to manage the Presley estate; they were Priscilla Presley, Elvis's accountant Joe Hanks, and the National Bank of Commerce in Memphis. Priscilla was involved in the management of the estate until her daughter Lisa Marie could inherit on 1 February 1993.

As reported by the *LA Times*, at that time Elvis's estate was valued at just $5 million and faced mounting bills for tax, insurance and 24-hour security for Elvis's grave.

The estate was generating an annual income of about $1 million in 1979, and, with no new albums or movies to release, that figure was expected to drop below $500,000.

Royalties from most of his old recordings went to RCA, which had bought the rights to them in 1973, rather than his estate. In the past whenever he needed money Elvis would just make a new recording or set out on another tour. Without him, something radical had to be done.

Working with a team of financial professionals, Priscilla formed Elvis Presley Enterprises (EPE), to manage all Elvis image rights and remaining royalties. The plans primarily included turning Graceland into a tourist attraction, which opened in 1982, and striking deals over Elvis's image, merchandising and royalties from songs recorded after the RCA deal.

Priscilla went on to gain fame in her own right in the 1980s when she worked as an actress on the popular primetime television series *Dallas*. She continues to promote Elvis, for example by making special appearances at some of the Royal Philharmonic live orchestral shows.

# Lisa Marie Presley

After the death of Minnie Mae in 1980, Lisa Marie became the sole beneficiary of Elvis's estate aged 13. She inherited on her 25th birthday in 1993, by which time the value of the estate had grown to an estimated $100 million.

Having worked with the estate for many years, in 2005 she sold 85 per cent of it, including Graceland. She works as a singer songwriter and has released four albums, since singing for the first time on the 20th anniversary of her father's death when she mixed her vocals with those of Elvis on his recording of *Don't Cry Daddy*.

She has been married four times, most famously to the actor Nicholas Cage and the 'prince of pop' Michael Jackson - the nearest rival to her father Elvis in terms of musical reputation and posthumous earnings.

Her daughter from her first marriage to musician Danny Keogh, Elvis's granddaughter Riley Keogh, is now a successful model and actress.

# Colonel Tom Parker

Parker lived for another 20 years after Elvis had died, eventually suffering a stroke and dying in hospital the next day, on 21 January 1997, in Las Vegas where he had lived since the 1980s.

In the first few years without Elvis, Parker continued to manage the estate. All its income, much of it from licensing contracts he had negotiated, would go to him, he would deduct his commission and send the rest to the estate. He also made money working as a consultant for Hilton Hotels and maintained a suite of rooms in their hotel in Las Vegas.

However, his reputation took a pounding in the early 1980s when he was involved in a court case brought by the trustees of the Elvis estate.

The matter came to a head unexpectedly in 1980 when, during a routine court review of estate management plans, Memphis probate judge Joseph W. Evans questioned the existing agreement between Parker and Elvis. He asked attorney Blanchard E. Tual, to investigate in order to protect the financial interests of Lisa Marie, a minor at the time.

Following an extensive review of the deals between Elvis and Parker, Tual found that Parker's management deal of 50% was extortionate, compared to the industry average of 15–20%, and said that since Elvis' death, Parker had 'violated his duty both to Elvis and to the estate . . . (by charging commissions) that were . . . excessive, imprudent . . . and beyond all reasonable bounds of industry standards.'

The principal charge against him involved the 1973 RCA deal which meant basically that Elvis's estate earned nothing from his main body of recordings, despite record sales during the year after his death alone being estimated as worth hundreds of millions of dollars. The report also accused Parker of failing to strike the best deals for Elvis during his lifetime and of not working to minimise his taxes, concluding that where Elvis 'was naïve, Parker was 'aggressive, shrewd and tough [with a] strong personality [which] dominated Elvis, his father and all others in Elvis' entourage.'

In his defence Parker said: 'Elvis and Vernon were well pleased with my services and desired to continue them over the years. Detailed explanations were regularly made of the transactions pertaining to Elvis and the companies.'

Nevertheless, the court directed lawyers to recover money from Parker and from RCA related to royalties outstanding on post-1973 recordings. The result was a 1983 settlement in which the estate was able to sever all ties with Parker and recover $1.1 million from RCA, which also agreed to continue payment of royalties on recordings made after March 1973. The estate still receives no royalties on the songs made before 1973, which are of course the most valuable recordings.

Despite this dispute, Parker maintained an association with Elvis, even appearing at events to honour Elvis in Memphis and the 1993 issue of an Elvis postage stamp. In 1994 he had a star dedicated to him on the Palm Springs Walk of Stars. But by this time Parker was a sick man, suffering various health issues. He wasn't seen in public for the last few years before his death.

As biographer Alanna Nash wrote in her book, *The Colonel*: "Whether regarded as a meretricious and evil confidence man, or as a brilliant marketer and strategist, as remarkable as the star he managed, no figure in all of entertainment is more controversial, colourful, or larger than life than Tom Parker'.

# Discography

## Studio Albums

| | | | |
|---|---|---|---|
| Elvis Presley | March 23rd 1956 | 1 (UK) | 1 (US) |
| Elvis | October 19th 1956 | 3 (UK) | 1( US) |
| Elvis Christmas Album | October 15th 1957 | 2 (UK) | 1 (US) |
| For LP Fans Only | February 6th 1959 | 19 (US) | |
| A Date With Elvis | July 24th 1959 | 4 (UK) | 32 (US) |
| Elvis is Back | April 8th 1960 | 1 (UK) | 2 (US) |
| His Hand in Mine | November 10th 1960 | 3 (UK) | 13 (US) |
| Something for Everybody | June 17th 1961 | 2 (UK) | 1 (US) |
| Pot Luck | June 5th 1962 | 1 (UK) | 4 (US) |
| How Great Thou Art | February 27th 1967 | 11 (UK) | 18 (US) |
| From Elvis in Memphis | June 17th 1969 | 1 (UK) | 13 (US) |
| From Memphis to Vegas / From Vegas to Memphis | October 14th 1969 | 3 (UK) | 12 (US) |
| Elvis Country (I'm 10,000 years old) | January 2nd 1971 | 6 (UK) | 12 (US) |
| Love Letters from Elvis | June 16th 1971 | 7 (UK) | 33 (US) |
| Elvis Sings The Wonderful World of Christmas | October 20th 1971 | | |
| Elvis Now | February 20th 1972 | 12 (UK) | 43 (US) |
| He Touched Me | April 1972 | 38 (UK) | 79 (US) |
| Elvis (The "Fool" Album) | July 1973 | 16 (UK) | 52 (US) |
| Raised on Rock / For Ol' Times Sake | October 1st 1973 | | 50 (US) |
| Good Times | March 20th 1974 | 42 (UK) | 90 (US) |
| Promised Land | January 8th 1975 | 21 (UK) | 47 (US) |
| Today | May 7th 1975 | 48 (UK) | 57 (US) |
| From Elvis Presley Boulevard Memphis Tennessee | May 1st 1976 | 29 (UK) | 41 (US) |
| Moody Blue | July 19th 1977 | 3 (UK) | 3 (US) |

## Live Albums

| | | | |
|---|---|---|---|
| From Memphis to Vegas / from Vegas to Memphis | October 14th 1969 | 3 (UK) | 12 (US) |
| On Stage | June 1970 | 2 (UK) | 13(US) |
| Elvis: as Recorded at Madison Square Garden | June 18th 1972 | 3 (UK) | 11 (US) |
| Aloha from Hawaii via Satellite | February 4th 1973 | 11 (UK) | 1 (US) |
| Elvis Recorded Live on Stage in Memphis | July 7th 1974 | 44( UK) | 33 (US) |
| Elvis in Concert | October 3rd 1977 | 13 (UK) | 5 (US) |

## Soundtrack Albums

| | | | |
|---|---|---|---|
| Loving You | July 1st 1957 | 1 (UK) | 1 (US) |
| King Creole | September 19th 1958 | 1 (UK) | 2 (US) |

| | | | |
|---|---|---|---|
| G.I. Blues | October 1st 1960 | 1 (UK) | 1 (US) |
| Blue Hawaii | November 9th 1962 | 1 (UK) | 1 (US) |
| Girls! Girls! Girls! | November 9th 1962 | 2 (UK) | 3 (US) |
| It Happened at the World's Fair | April 10th 1963 | 4 (UK) | 4 (US) |
| Fun in Acapulco | November 1st 1963 | 9 (UK) | 3 (US) |
| Kissin' Cousins | April 2nd 1964 | 5 (UK) | 6 (US |
| Roustabout | October 20th 1964 | 12 (UK) | 1 (US) |
| Girl Happy | March 2nd 1965 | 8 (UK) | 8 (US) |
| Harum Scarum | November 3rd 1965 | 11 (UK) | 8 (US) |
| Frankie and Johnny | March 1st 1966 | 11 (UK) | 20 (US) |
| Paradise, Hawaiian Style | June 10th 1966 | 7 (UK) | 15 (US) |
| Spinout | October 31st 1966 | 17 (UK) | 18 (US) |
| Double Trouble | June 1st 1967 | 34 (UK) | 47 (US) |
| Clambake | October 10th 1967 | 39 (UK) | 40 (US) |
| Speedway | May 1st 1968 | | 82 (US) |
| Elvis (NBC-TV Special) | November 22nd 1968 | 2 (UK) | 8 (US) |
| That's the Way It Is | November 11th 1970 | 12 (UK) | 21 (US) |
| Viva Elvis | November 11th 2010 | 19 (UK) | 48 (US) |

Music by Elvis continues to sell. Since his death many 'Elvis' albums have been released, including 115 posthumous compilations and 11 remix albums.

## Singles - US Billboard Hot 100

**1954**

That's All Right
Good Rockin' Tonight
I Don't Care If the Sun Don't Shine — 74 (US Hot)

**1955**

Baby Let's Play House
Mystery Train
I Forgot to Remember to Forget

**1956**

Heartbreak Hotel — 1 (US Hot)
I Was the One — 19 (US Hot)
Blue Suede Shoes — 20 (US Hot)
I Want to, I Need You, I Love You — 1 (US Hot)
My Baby Left Me — 31 (US Hot)
Don't Be Cruel — 1 (US Hot)
Hound Dog — 1 (US Hot)
Tutti-Frutti
I Got a Woman
I'll Never Let You Go (Lil' Darlin')
I Love You Because

Blue Moon — 55 (US Hot)
Money Honey — 76 (US Hot)
Shake Rattle and Roll
Love Me Tender — 1 (US Hot)
Any Way You Want Me — 27 (US Hot)
Love Me — 2 (US Hot)
When My Blue Moon Turns to Gold Again — 19 (US Hot)
Paralysed — 59 (US Hot)
Old Shep — 47 (US Hot)
Poor Boy — 24 (US Hot)

**1957**

Too Much — 1 (US Hot)
Playing for Keeps — 21 (US Hot)
All Shook Up — 1 (US Hot)
That's When Your Heartaches Begin — 58 (US Hot)
Peace in the Valley — 25 (US Hot)
(Let Me Be Your) Teddy Bear — 1 (US Hot)
Loving You — 20 (US Hot)
Mean Woman Blues
Jailhouse Rock — 1 (US Hot)
Treat Me Nice — 18 (US Hot)

## 1958

| | |
|---|---|
| Don't | 1 (US Hot) |
| I Beg of You | 8 (US Hot) |
| Wear My Ring around Your Neck | 2 (US Hot) |
| Doncha' Think It's Time | 15 (US Hot) |
| Hardheaded Woman | 1 (US Hot) |
| Don't Ask Me Why | 25 (US Hot) |
| One Night | 4 (US Hot) |
| I Got Stung | 8 (US Hot) |

## 1959

| | |
|---|---|
| (Now and Then There's) A Fool Such As I | 2 (US Hot) |
| I Need Your Love Tonight | 4 (US Hot) |
| A Big Hunk o' Love | 1 (US Hot) |
| My Wish Came True | 12 (US Hot) |

## 1960

| | |
|---|---|
| Stuck on You | 1 (US Hot) |
| Fame and Fortune | 17 (US Hot) |
| It's Now or Never | 1 (US Hot) |
| A Mess of Blues | 32 (US Hot) |
| Are You Lonesome Tonight | 1 (US Hot) |
| I Gotta Know | 20 (US Hot) |

## 1961

| | |
|---|---|
| Surrender | 1 (US Hot) |
| Lonely Man | 32 (US Hot) |
| Flaming Star | 14 (US Hot) |
| I Feel so Bad | 5 (US Hot) |
| Wild in the Country | 26 (US Hot) |
| (Marie's the Name) His Latest Flame | 4 (US Hot) |
| Little Sister | 5 (US Hot) |
| Can't Help Falling in Love | 2 (US Hot) |

## 1962

| | |
|---|---|
| Rock-a-Hula Baby | 23 (US Hot) |
| Good Luck Charm | 1 (US Hot) |
| Anything That's Part of You | 31 (US Hot) |
| Follow That Dream | 15 (US Hot) |
| She's Not You | 5 (US Hot) |
| Just Tell Her Jim Said Hello | 55 (US Hot) |
| King of the Whole Wide World | 30 (US Hot) |
| Return to Sender | 2 (US Hot) |
| Where Do You Come From | 99 (US Hot) |

## 1963

| | |
|---|---|
| One Broken Heart for Sale | 11 (US Hot) |

| | |
|---|---|
| They Remind Me Too Much of You | 53 (US Hot) |
| (You're the Devil in Disguise) | 3 (US Hot) |
| Bossa Nova Baby | 8 (US Hot) |
| Witchcraft | 32 (US Hot) |

## 1964

| | |
|---|---|
| Kissin' Cousins | 12 (US Hot) |
| It Hurts Me | 29 (US Hot) |
| Kiss Me Quick | 34 (US Hot) |
| Suspicion | 103 (US Hot) |
| What'd I Say | 21 (US Hot) |
| Viva Las Vegas | 29 (US Hot) |
| Such a Night | 16 (US Hot) |
| Never-Ending | 111 (US Hot) |
| Ask Me | 12 (US Hot) |
| Ain't That Loving You Baby | 16 (US Hot) |
| Wooden Heart | 107 (US Hot) |

## 1965

| | |
|---|---|
| Do the Clam | 21 (US Hot) |
| You'll Be Gone | 121 (US Hot) |
| Crying in the Chapel | 3 (US Hot) |
| (Such An) Easy Question | 11 (US Hot) |
| It Feels so Right | 55 (US Hot) |
| I'm Yours | 11 (US Hot) |
| Puppet on a String | 14 (US Hot) |
| Santa Claus Is Back in Town | |

## 1966

| | |
|---|---|
| Tell Me Why | 33 (US Hot) |
| Blue River | 95 (US Hot) |
| Joshua Fit the Battle | |
| Milky White Way | |
| Frankie and Johnny | 25 (US Hot) |
| Please Don't Stop Loving Me | 45 (US Hot) |
| Love Letters | 19 (US Hot) |
| Come What May | 109 (US Hot) |
| 'Spinout | 40 (US Hot) |
| All That I Am | 41 (US Hot) |
| If Every Day Was Like Christmas | |

## 1967

| | |
|---|---|
| Indescribably Blue | 33 (US Hot) |
| Fools Fall in Love | 102 (US Hot) |
| Long Legged Girl (With the Short Dress On) | 63 (US Hot) |
| That's Someone You Never Forget | 92 (US Hot) |
| There's Always Me | 56 (US Hot) |

| | |
|---|---|
| Judy | 78 (US Hot) |
| Big Boss Man | 38 (US Hot) |
| You Don't Know Me | 44 (US Hot) |

### 1968

| | |
|---|---|
| Guitar Man | 43 (US Hot) |
| Hi-Heel Sneakers | |
| U.S. Male | 28 (US Hot) |
| Stay Away | 67 (US Hot) |
| You'll Never Walk Alone | 90 (US Hot) |
| We Call on Him | 106 (US Hot) |
| Your Time Hasn't Come Yet Baby | 72 (US Hot) |
| Let Yourself Go | 71 (US Hot) |
| A Little Less Conversation | 69 (US Hot) |
| Almost in Love | 95 (US Hot) |
| If I Can Dream | 12 (US Hot) |
| Edge of Reality | 112 (US Hot) |

### 1969

| | |
|---|---|
| Memories | 35 (US Hot) |
| How Great Thou Art | 101 (US Hot) |
| In the Ghetto | 3 (US Hot) |
| Clean Up Your Own Backyard | 35 (US Hot) |
| Suspicious Minds | 1 (US Hot) |
| Don't Cry Daddy | 6 (US Hot) |
| Rubberneckin' | |

### 1970

| | |
|---|---|
| Kentucky Rain | 16 (US Hot) |
| The Wonder of You | 9 (US Hot) |
| Mama Liked the Roses | |
| I've Lost You | 32 (US Hot) |
| The Next Step is Love | |
| You Don't Have to Say You Love Me | 11 (US Hot) |
| Patch It Up | |
| I Really Don't Want to Know | 21 (US Hot) |
| There Goes My Everything | |

### 1971

| | |
|---|---|
| Rags to Riches | |
| Where Did They Go, Lord | 33 (US Hot) |
| Life | 53 (US Hot) |
| Only Believe | |
| I'm Leavin' | 36 (US Hot) |
| Heart of Rome | |
| It's Only Love | 51 (US Hot) |
| The Sound of Your Cry | |

| | |
|---|---|
| Merry Christmas Baby | |

### 1972

| | |
|---|---|
| Until It's Time for You to go | 40 (US Hot) |
| We Can Make the Morning | |
| He Touched Me | |
| An American Trilogy | |
| Burning Love | 2 (US Hot) |
| It's a Matter of Time | |
| Separate Ways | 20 (US Hot) |
| Always on my Mind | |

### 1973

| | |
|---|---|
| Steamroller Blues | 17 (US Hot) |
| Fool | |
| Raised on Rock | 41 (US Hot) |
| For Ol' Times Sake | |

### 1974

| | |
|---|---|
| I've Got a Thing About You Baby | 39 (US Hot) |
| Take Good Care of Her | |
| If You Talk in Your Sleep | 17 (US Hot) |
| Help Me | |
| Promised Land | 14 (US Hot) |
| It's Midnight | |

### 1975

| | |
|---|---|
| T-R-O-U-B-L-E | 35 (US Hot) |
| Bringing it Back | 65 (US Hot) |
| Pieces of My Life | |

### 1976

| | |
|---|---|
| Hurt | 28 (US Hot) |
| For the Heart | |
| Moody Blue | 31 (US Hot) |
| She Thinks I Still Care | |

### 1977

| | |
|---|---|
| Way Down | 18 (US Hot) |
| Pledging My Love | |
| My Way | 22 (US Hot) |
| America | |

### 1978

| | |
|---|---|
| Unchained Melody | |
| Softly As I Leave You | 109 (US Hot) |

# Concert appearances

All USA except where specified

## 1977

### JUNE

| | | |
|---|---|---|
| 26 | Market Square Arena | Indianapolis, Indiana |
| 25 | River Front Coliseum | Cincinnati, Ohio |
| 24 | Veterans Memorial Coliseum | Madison, Wisconsin |
| 23 | Veterans Memorial Auditorium | Des Moines, Iowa |
| 22 | Sioux Falls Arena | Sioux Falls, South Dakota |
| 21 | Mount Rushmore | Cheyenne, Wyoming |
| 21 | Rushmore Plaza Civic Centre Arena | Rapid City, South Dakota |
| 20 | Pershing Auditorium | Lincoln, Nebraska |
| 19 | Omaha Civic Auditorium | Omaha, Nebraska |
| 18 | Kemper Arena | Kansas City, Missouri |
| 17 | Southwest Missouri State University | Springfield, Missouri |
| 02 | - | Mobile, Alabama |
| 01 | Macon Centreplex Coliseum | Atlanta, Georgia |

### MAY

| | | |
|---|---|---|
| 31 | Louisiana State University | Baton Rouge, Louisiana |
| 30 | Vystar Veterans Memorial Arena | Jacksonville, Florida |
| 29 | Royal Farms Arena | Baltimore, Maryland |
| 28 | The Spectrum | Philadelphia, Pennsylvania |
| 27 | Veterans Memorial Arena | Rochester, New York |
| 26 | Veterans Memorial Arena | Rochester, New York |
| 25 | Rochester Community War Memorial | Rochester, New York |
| 24 | William B. Bell Auditorium | Augusta, Georgia |
| 23 | Providence Civic Center | Providence, Rhode Island |
| 22 | Capital Center | Washington D.C. |
| 21 | Kentucky State Fair & Expo Center | Louisville, Kentucky |
| 20 | Stokely Athletic Center, University | Knoxville. Tennessee |
| 03 | Dow Event Center | Detroit, Michigan |
| 01/02 | Chicago Stadium | Chicago, Illinois |

### APRIL

| | | |
|---|---|---|
| 30 | Mayo Civic Centre | Minneapolis, Minnesota |
| 30 | St. Paul Civic Centre | Saint Paul, Minnesota |
| 29 | Duluth Entertainment Conv Center | Minneapolis, Minnesota |
| 28 | Brown County Arena | Green Bay, Wisconsin |
| 27 | UW-Milwaukee Panther Arena | Milwaukee, Wisconsin |
| 26 | Wings Stadium | Grand Rapids, Michigan |
| 25 | Dow Event Center | Detroit, Michigan |
| 24 | Chrisler Arena | Detroit, Michigan |
| 23 | University of Toledo | Toledo, Ohio |
| 22 | Olympia Stadium | Detroit, Michigan |
| 21 | Greensboro Coliseum | Greensboro, North Carolina |
| 03 | - | Jacksonville, Florida |
| 02 | - | Atlanta, Georgia |
| 01 | - | Mobile, Alabama |

### MARCH

| | | |
|---|---|---|
| 31 | - | Baton Rouge, Louisiana |
| 29/30 | Rapides Parish Coliseum | Baton Rouge, Louisiana |

| | | |
|---|---|---|
| 28 | Austin Municipal Auditorium | Austin, Texas |
| 27 | Taylor County Coliseum | Dallas, Texas |
| 22 | Taylor County Coliseum | Abilene, Texas |
| 25/26 | University of Oklahoma | Oklahoma City, Oklahoma |
| 24 | Amarillo Civic Center | Amarillo, Texas |
| 23 | Arizona State University | Phoenix, Arizona |

### FEBRUARY

| | | |
|---|---|---|
| 20/21 | Charlotte Coliseum | Charlotte, North Carolina |
| 19 | Freedom Hall Civic Centre | Johnson City, Tennessee |
| 19 | Freedom Hall Civic Centre | Knoxville, Tennessee |
| 18 | Carolina Coliseum | Columbia, South Carolina |
| 17 | Savannah Civic Center | Augusta, Georgia |
| 16 | Garrett Coliseum | Montgomery, Alabama |
| 15 | Sports Stadium | Orlando, Florida |
| 14 | Bayfront Center Arena | St. Petersburg, Florida |
| 13 | Auditorium | Fort Lauderdale, Florida |
| 12 | Hollywood Sportatorium | Fort Lauderdale, Florida |

**Typical 1977 set list**

| | |
|---|---|
| See See Rider Blues | Fever |
| I've Got a Woman | How Great Thou Art |
| Amen | Early Morning Rain |
| Love Me | What'd I Say |
| If You Love Me (Let Me Know) | Johnny B. Goode |
| You Gave Me a Mountain | School Day (Ring Ring Goes the Bell) |
| Jailhouse Rock | Hurt |
| 'O sole mio' | Hound Dog |
| It's Now or Never | Danny Boy |
| Tryin' to Get to You | Walk With Me |
| That's All Right | Blue Suede Shoes |
| Are You Lonesome Tonight? | Lawdy Miss Clawdy |
| My Way | Can't Help Falling in Love |

## 1976

### DECEMBER

| | | |
|---|---|---|
| 31 | Mellon Arena | Pittsburgh, Pennsylvania |
| 30 | The Omni (Omni Coliseum) | Atlanta, Georgia |
| 29 | Civic Center | Birmingham, Alabama |
| 28 | Kay Bailey Hutchison Conv Center | Dallas, Texas |
| 27 | Wichita State University | Wichita, Kansas |
| 02-12 | Hilton Theater | Las Vegas, Nevada |

### NOVEMBER

| | | |
|---|---|---|
| 30 | Anaheim Convention Center | Los Angeles, California |
| 28/29 | Cow Palace | San Francisco, California |
| 27 | McArthur Court, University of Oregon | Salem, Oregon |
| 26 | Coliseum | Portland, Oregon |
| 25 | McArthur Court, University of Oregon | Salem, Oregon |
| 24 | Centennial Coliseum | Reno, Nevada |

## OCTOBER

| | | |
|---|---|---|
| 27 | Southern Illinois University | St Louis, Missouri |
| 26 | University of Dayton | Dayton, Ohio |
| 25 | Allen County War Memorial Coliseum | Fort Wayne, Indiana |
| 24 | Roberts Stadium | Louisville, Kentucky |
| 23 | Cleveland Coliseum | Cleveland, Ohio |
| 22 | University of Illinois | Champaign, Illinois |
| 21 | Wings Stadium | Grand Rapids, Michigan |
| 20 | University of Notre Dame | Notre Dame, Indiana |
| 19 | Veterans Memorial Coliseum | Madison, Wisconsin |
| 18 | Sioux Falls Arena | Sioux Falls, South Dakota |
| 17 | Metropolitan Sport Center | Minneapolis, Minnesota |
| 16 | Duluth Entertainment Center | Minneapolis, Minnesota |
| 15 | Chicago Stadium | Chicago, Illinois |
| 14 | - | Kalamazoo, Michigan |

## SEPTEMBER

| | | |
|---|---|---|
| 07/08 | Pine Bluff Convention Center | Little Rock, Arkansas |
| 06 | Von Braun Center Arena | Huntsville. Alabama |
| 05 | Mississippi Coliseum | Jackson, Mississippi |
| 04 | Jenkins Arena, RP Funding Center | Tampa, Florida |
| 03 | Bayfront Center Arena | St. Petersburg, Florida |
| 02 | Curtis Hixon Hall | Tampa, Florida |
| 01 | Vystar Veterans Memorial Arena | Jacksonville, Florida |

## AUGUST

| | | |
|---|---|---|
| 3 | Macon Centerplex Coliseum | Atlanta, Georgia |
| 30 | Ferguson Center Ballroom, | Birmingham, Alabama |
| 29 | Bayfront Auditorium | Mobile, Alabama |
| 28 | Hofheinz Pavilion | Houston, Texas |
| 27 | HemisFair Arena | San Antonio, Texas |
| 03-05 | Cumberland Mem. Auditorium | Fayetteville, North Carolina |
| 02 | RKECivic Center | Winston-Salem North Carolina |
| 01 | Hampton Coliseum | Newport News, Virginia |

## JULY

| | | |
|---|---|---|
| 31 | Hampton Coliseum | Newport News, Virginia |
| 30 | New Haven Veterans Mem. Coliseum | Bridgeport, Connecticut |
| 29 | XL Center | Springfield, Massachusetts |
| 28 | Hartford Civic Center | Hartford, Connecticut |
| 26/27 | Rochester War Memorial | Rochester, New York |
| 25 | War Memorial, Oncenter Complex | Rochester, New York |
| 23 | Kentucky State Fair & Expo Center | Louisville, Kentucky |
| 05 | Mid-South Coliseum | Memphis, Tennessee |
| 04 | Mabee Center | Tulsa, Oklahoma |
| 03 | Tarrant County Convention Center | Fort Worth, Texas |
| 02 | Louisiana State University | Baton Rouge, Louisiana |
| 01 | Hirsch Memorial Coliseum | Shreveport, Louisiana |

## JUNE

| | | |
|---|---|---|
| 30 | Greensboro Coliseum Complex | Greensboro, North Carolina |
| 29 | Richmond Coliseum | Richmond, Virginia |
| 28 | Wachovia Spectrum Center | Philadelphia, Pennsylvania |
| 27 | Capital Center | Largo, Maryland |
| 26 | Providence Civic Center | Providence, Rhode Island |
| 25 | Buffalo Memorial Auditorium | Buffalo, New York |

| | | |
|---|---|---|
| 04-06 | The Omni (Omni Coliseum) | Atlanta, Georgia |
| 03 | Fort Worth Convention Center | Dallas, Texas |
| 02 | Civic Center Grand Hall | El Paso, Texas |
| 01 | Tucson Convention Center | Tucson, Arizona |

## MAY

| | | |
|---|---|---|
| 31 | Lubbock Municipal Auditorium | Lubbock, Texas |
| 30 | Ector County Coliseum | Lubbock, Texas |
| 29 | Myriad | Oklahoma City, Oklahoma |
| 28 | Iowa State University | Des Moines, Iowa |
| 27 | Indiana State University | Indianapolis, Indiana |
| 09-01 | Sahara Tahoe Hotel | Reno, Nevada |

## APRIL

| | | |
|---|---|---|
| 30 | Sahara Tahoe Hotel | Reno, Nevada |
| 27 | Spokane Arena | Spokane, Washington |
| 26 | Climate Pledge Arena | Seattle, Washington |
| 25 | Long Beach Arena | Los Angeles, California |
| 24 | Valley View Casino Center | San Diego, California |
| 23 | McNichols Sports Arena | Denver, Colorado |
| 22 | Omaha Civic Auditorium | Omaha, Nebraska |
| 22 | Omaha Auditorium Arena | Omaha, Nebraska |
| 21 | Kemper Arena | Kansas City, Missouri |

## MARCH

| | | |
|---|---|---|
| 22 | Henry W. Kiel Municipal Auditorium | St. Louis, Missouri |
| 21 | Riverfront Coliseum | Cincinnati, Ohio |
| 20 | Charlotte Coliseum | Charlotte, North Carolina |
| 19-17 | Freedom Hall Civic Center | Knoxville, Tennessee |

# 1975

## DECEMBER

| | | |
|---|---|---|
| 31 | Pontiac Silverdome | Detroit, Michigan |
| 15-02 | Hilton Theater | Las Vegas, Nevada |

## OCTOBER

| | | |
|---|---|---|
| 17 | St. Paul Civic Center | St. Paul, Minnesota |

## AUGUST

| | | |
|---|---|---|
| 20-18 | Hilton Theater | Las Vegas, Nevada |

## JULY

| | | |
|---|---|---|
| 24/23 | US Cellular Center | Knoxville, Tennessee |
| 22 | Asheville Civic Center | Asheville, North Carolina |
| 21 | Greensboro Coliseum Complex | Greensboro, North Carolina |
| 20 | Scope | Norfolk, Virginia |
| 19 | NYCB Live: Nassau VMC* | New York, New York |
| 18 | Richfield Coliseum | Richfield, Ohio |
| 17/16 | New Haven VMC* | Bridgeport, Connecticut |
| 15/14 | Springfield C. Center | Springfield, Massachusetts |
| 13 | Buffalo Niagara Convention Centre | Buffalo, New York |
| 12/11 | Charleston Civic Center | Charleston, West Virginia |
| 10 | Cleveland Coliseum | Cleveland, Ohio |
| 09 | ISU Hulman Center | Indianapolis, Indiana |
| 08 | Cox Convention Center | Oklahoma City, Oklahoma |

*VMC Veterans Memorial Coliseum       *CC Convention Centre       *SU State University

**JUNE**

| | | |
|---|---|---|
| 10 | Mid-South Coliseum | Memphis, Tennessee |
| 09/08 | Mississippi Colosseum | Jackson, Mississippi |
| 07 | Hirsch Memorial Colosseum | Shreveport, Louisiana |
| 06 | Kay Bailey Hutchison CC* | Dallas, Texas |
| 05/04 | Hofheinz Pavilion | Houston Texas |
| 03 | University of Alabama | Birmingham, Alabama |
| 02 | Bayfront Auditorium | Mobile, Alabama |
| 01 | Von Braun Center Arena | Huntsville, Alabama |

**MAY**

| | | |
|---|---|---|
| 31-30 | Von Braun Center Arena | Huntsville, Alabama |
| 07/06 | Middle Tennessee State University | Nashville, Tennessee |
| 05 | Mississippi Colosseum | Jackson, Mississippi |
| 04 | Lake Charles Civic Center | Lake Charles, Louisiana |
| 03 | Monroe Civic Centre | - |
| 02/01 | The Omni (Omni Coliseum) | Atlanta, Georgia |

**APRIL**

| | | |
|---|---|---|
| 30 | The Omni (Omni Coliseum) | Atlanta, Georgia |
| 29 | Middle Tennessee State University | Nashville, Tennessee |
| 28/27 | R P Funding Center | Tampa, Florida |
| 26 | Curtis Hixon Hall | Tampa, Florida |
| 25 | Vystar Veterans Memorial Arena | Jacksonville, Florida |
| 24 | Macon Centreplex Colosseum | Atlanta, Georgia |
| 01 | Hilton Theater | Las Vegas, Nevada |

**MARCH**

| | | |
|---|---|---|
| 31-18 | Hilton Theater | Las Vegas, Nevada |

**1974**

**OCTOBER**

| | | |
|---|---|---|
| 14/11 | Sahara Tahoe Hotel | Reno, Nevada |
| 09 | Exposition Center | Dallas, Texas |
| 08 | HemisFair Arena | San Antonio, Texas |
| 07 | Henry Levitt Arena, Wichita SU* | Wichita, Kansas |
| 06 | University of Dayton | Dayton, Ohio |
| 05 | Indianapolis Convention Center | Indianapolis, Indiana |
| 05 | The Expo Center | Indianapolis, Indiana |
| 04 | Olympia Stadium | Detroit, Michigan |
| 03/02 | Mayo Civic Center | Minneapolis, Minnesota |
| 01 | University of Notre Dame | Notre Dame, Indiana |

**SEPTEMBER**

| | | |
|---|---|---|
| 30 | University of Notre Dame | Notre Dame, Indiana |
| 29 | Olympia Stadium | Detroit, Michigan |
| 28/27 | College Park Field House | Baltimore, Maryland |
| 02/01 | Hilton Theater | Las Vegas, Nevada |

**AUGUST**

| | | |
|---|---|---|
| 31-19 | Hilton Theater | Las Vegas, Nevada |

**JULY**

| | | |
|---|---|---|
| 02 | Salt Palace Convention Center | Salt Lake City, Utah |
| 01 | Omaha Civic Auditorium | Omaha, Nebraska |

| | | |
|---|---|---|
| 30 | Omaha Civic Auditorium | Omaha, Nebraska |
| 29 | Municipal Auditorium | Kansas City, Missouri |
| 28 | UW-Milwaukee Panther Arena | Milwaukee, Wisconsin |
| 27 | Assembly Hall | Bloomington, Indiana |
| 25 | St. John Arena | Columbus, Ohio |
| 24 | Buffalo Niagara Convention Center | Buffalo, New York |
| 23 | The Spectrum | Philadelphia, Pennsylvania |
| 22 | Providence Civic Center | Providence, Rhode Island |
| 21 | Cleveland Convention Centre | Cleveland, Ohio |
| 20 | Veterans Memorial Auditorium | Des Moines, Iowa |
| 19 | Amarillo Civic Center | Amarillo, Texas |
| 18/17 | Louisiana State University | Baton Rouge, Louisiana |
| 16 | Fort Worth Convention Center | Dallas, Texas |
| 15 | Tarrant County Convention Center | Fort Worth, Texas |

**MAY**

| | | |
|---|---|---|
| 27-16 | Sahara Tahoe Hotel | Reno, Nevada |
| 13 | Swing Auditorium | Los Angeles, California |
| 12 | Selland Arena | Fresno, California |
| 11 | The Forum | Los Angeles, California |
| 10 | Swing Auditorium | Los Angeles, California |

**MARCH**

| | | |
|---|---|---|
| 20 | Mid-South Coliseum | Memphis, Tennessee |
| 19 | Middle Tennessee State University | Nashville, Tennessee |
| 18 | Richmond Coliseum | Richmond, Virginia |
| 17/16 | Mid-South Coliseum | Memphis, Tennessee |
| 15 | Middle Tennessee State University | Nashville, Tennessee |
| 14 | Middle Tennessee State University | Nashville, Tennessee |
| 13 | Greensboro Coliseum Complex | Greensboro, North Carolina |
| 12 | Richmond Coliseum | Richmond, Virginia |
| 11 | - | Lakeland, Florida |
| 11 | Hampton Coliseum | Newport News, Virginia |
| 10 | RKE Civic Center | Winston-Salem, North Carolina |
| 09 | Charlotte Coliseum | Charlotte, North Carolina |
| 08/07 | Monroe Civic Center Arena | Shreveport, Louisiana |
| 06 | Garrett Coliseum | Montgomery, Alabama |
| 05 | Beard-Eaves Memorial Coliseum | Columbus, Georgia |
| 04 | Monroe Civic Center Arena | Shreveport, Louisiana |
| 03 | Astrodome | Houston, Texas |
| 02/01 | Oral Roberts University | Tulsa, Oklahoma |

**FEBRUARY**

| | | |
|---|---|---|
| 09-01 | Hilton Theater | Las Vegas, Nevada |

**JANUARY**

| | | |
|---|---|---|
| 31-26 | Hilton Theater | Las Vegas, Nevada |

**1973**

**SEPTEMBER**

| | | |
|---|---|---|
| 03-01 | Hilton Theater | Las Vegas, Nevada |

**AUGUST**

| | | |
|---|---|---|
| 31-06 | Hilton Theater | Las Vegas, Nevada |

## JULY

03 The Omni (Omni Coliseum)          Atlanta, Georgia
02 Cox Convention Center             Oklahoma City, Oklahoma
01 Nashville Municipal Auditorium    Nashville, Tennessee

## JUNE

30/29 The Omni (Omni Coliseum)           Atlanta, Georgia
28 Henry W. Kiel Municipal Auditorium    St. Louis, Missouri
27 Cincinnati Gardens                    Cincinnati, Ohio
26-24 Mellon Arena                       Pittsburgh, Pennsylvania
23 NYCB Live: Nassau VMC*                New York, New York
22 Nassau Coliseum                       Uniondale, New York
21 The Omni (Omni Coliseum)              Atlanta, Georgia
20 Bayfront Auditorium                   Mobile, Alabama

## MAY

20-04 Sahara Tahoe Hotel             Reno, Nevada

## APRIL

30 Denver Coliseum                          Denver, Colorado
29 Mercer Arena                             Seattle, Washington
28 Spokane Arena                            Spokane, Washington
27 Veterans Memorial Coliseum               Portland, Oregon
26 Valley View Casino Center                San Diego, California
25 Selland Arena                            Fresno, California
24/23 Los Angeles Convention Center         Los Angeles, California
22 Arizona Veterans Memorial Coliseum       Phoenix, Arizona

## FEBRUARY

23-01 Hilton Theater                 Las Vegas. Nevada

## JANUARY

31-26 Hilton Theater                 Las Vegas. Nevada
14 Honolulu International Center     Honolulu, Hawaii
12 Honolulu International Center     Honolulu, Hawaii

### Madison Square Garden 1972 set list

| | |
|---|---|
| That's All Right | Don't Be Cruel |
| Proud Mary | Love Me Tender |
| Never Been to Spain | Blue Suede Shoes |
| Until It's Time for You to Go | Hound Dog |
| You Don't Have to Say You Love Me | Bridge Over Troubled Water |
| Polk Salad Annie | Suspicious Minds |
| Love Me | For the Good Times |
| All Shook Up | An American Trilogy |
| Heartbreak Hotel | Funny How Time Slips Away |
| (Let Me Be) Your Teddy Bear | Can't Help Falling in Love |

## 1972

### NOVEMBER

18/17 Honolulu International Center      Honolulu, Hawaii
15/14 Long Beach Arena                   Los Angeles, California
11 O.co Coliseum                         San Francisco, California
10 El Paso County Coliseum               El Paso, Texas
09 Tucson Convention Center              Tucson, Arizona

08 City Bank Coliseum                Lubbock, Texas

## SEPTEMBER

04-01 Hilton Theater                 Las Vegas, Nevada

## AUGUST

31-04 Hilton Theater                 Las Vegas, Nevada

## JUNE

20 Assembly Center                       Tulsa, Oklahoma
19 Henry Levitt Arena, Wichita SU*       Wichita, Kansas
18 Tarrant County Convention Center      Fort Worth, Texas
17/16 Chicago Stadium                    Chicago, Illinois
15 Auditorium                            Milwaukee, Wisconsin
14 UW-Milwaukee Panther Arena            Milwaukee, Wisconsin
13 Robert's Stadium                      Evansville, Indiana
12 Allen County WMC*                     Fort Wayne, Texas
11-09 Madison Square Garden              New York, New York

## APRIL

19 Tingley Coliseum                      Albuquerque, New Mexico
18 HemisFair Arena                       San Antonio, Texas
17 Barton Coliseum                       Little Rock, Arkansas
16 Vystar Veterans Memorial Arena        Jacksonville, Florida
15 Macon Centreplex Coliseum             Atlanta, Georgia
14 Greenboro Coliseum Complex            Greensboro North Carolina
13 Charlotte Coliseum                    Charlotte, North Carolina
12 Pepsi Coliseum                        Indianapolis, Indiana
11 RKE Civic Center                      Winston-Salem, North Carolina
10 Richmond Coliseum                     Richmond, Virginia
09 Hampton Coliseum                      Newport News, Virginia
08 University of Tennessee               Knoxville, Tennessee
07 University of Dayton Arena            Dayton, Ohio
06 Olympia Stadium                       Detroit, Michigan
05 Buffalo Memorial Auditorium           Buffalo, New York

## FEBRUARY

23-01 Hilton Theater                 Las Vegas, Nevada

## JANUARY

31-26 Hilton Theater                 Las Vegas, Nevada

## 1971

### NOVEMBER

16 Salt Palace Convention Center         Salt Lake City, Utah
15 Municipal Auditorium                  Kansas City, Missouri
14 University of Alabama                 Birmingham, Alabama
13 Dallas Memorial Centre                Dallas, Texas
12 Hofheinz Pavilion                     Houston, Texas
11 Cincinnati Gardens                    Cincinnati, Ohio
10 Boston Garden                         Boston, Massachusetts
08 The Spectrum                          Philadelphia, Pennsylvania
06 Public Auditorium                     Cleveland, Ohio
05 Metropolitan Sports Centre            Minneapolis, Minnesota
04-01 Hilton Theater                     Las Vegas, Hilton

**AUGUST**

| | | |
|---|---|---|
| 31-09 | Hilton Theater | Las Vegas, Hilton |
| 02-01 | Sahara Tahoe Hotel | Reno, Nevada |

**JULY**

| | | |
|---|---|---|
| 31-20 | Sahara Tahoe Hotel | Reno, Nevada |

**FEBRUARY**

| | | |
|---|---|---|
| 23-01 | The International Hotel | Las Vegas, Nevada |

**JANUARY**

| | | |
|---|---|---|
| 31-26 | The International Hotel | Las Vegas, Nevada |

## 1970

**NOVEMBER**

| | | |
|---|---|---|
| 15 | Sports Arena | San Diego, California |
| 14 | The Forum | Los Angeles, California |
| 13 | Cow Palace | San Francisco, California |
| 12 | Climate Pledge Arena | Seattle, Washington |
| 11 | Veterans Memorial Coliseum | Portland, Oregon |
| 10 | O.co Coliseum | San Francisco, California |

**SEPTEMBER**

| | | |
|---|---|---|
| 17 | Denver Coliseum | Denver, Colorado |
| 16 | Oklahoma State Fair Arena | Oklahoma City Oklahoma |
| 15 | Valley View Casino Center | San Diego, California |
| 13 | Curtis Hixon Hall | Tampa, Florida |
| 12 | Olympia Stadium | Detroit, Michigan |
| 10 | Henry W. Kiel Municipal Auditorium | St. Louis, Missouri |
| 09 | Arizona VMC* | Phoenix, Arizona |
| 07-01 | The International Hotel | Las Vegas, Nevada |

**AUGUST**

| | | |
|---|---|---|
| 31-10 | The International Hotel | Las Vegas, Nevada |

**MARCH**

| | | |
|---|---|---|
| 01 | The Astrodome | Houston, Texas |

**FEBRUARY**

| | | |
|---|---|---|
| 28-27 | The Astrodome | Houston, Texas |
| 23-01 | The International Hotel | Las Vegas, Nevada |

**JANUARY**

| | | |
|---|---|---|
| 31-26 | The International Hotel | Las Vegas, Nevada |

## 1969

**SEPTEMBER**

| | | |
|---|---|---|
| 02 | Baltimore Civic Center | Baltimore, Maryland |

**AUGUST**

| | | |
|---|---|---|
| 28-01 | The International Hotel | Las Vegas, Nevada |

**JULY**

| | | |
|---|---|---|
| 31 | The International Hotel | Las Vegas, Nevada |

## 1961

**MARCH**

| | | |
|---|---|---|
| 25 | Bloch Arena Pearl Harbour | Honolulu, Hawaii |

**FEBRUARY**

| | | |
|---|---|---|
| 25 | Ellis Auditorium (North Music Hall) | Memphis, Tennessee |

## 1960

**MARCH**

| | | |
|---|---|---|
| 25 | Bloch Arena Pearl Harbour | Honolulu, Hawaii |

## 1957

**NOVEMBER**

| | | |
|---|---|---|
| 11 | Schofield Barracks | Honolulu, Hawaii |
| 10 | Honolulu Stadium | Honolulu, Hawaii |

**OCTOBER**

| | | |
|---|---|---|
| 29/28 | Pan Pacific Auditorium | Los Angeles, California |
| 27 | Oakland Auditorium | San Francisco, California |
| 26 | San Jose Civic | San Francisco, California |

**SEPTEMBER**

| | | |
|---|---|---|
| 27 | Fairground | Memphis, Tennessee |
| 02 | Multnomah Stadium | Portland, Oregon |
| 01 | Sicks' Stadium | Seattle, Washington |

**AUGUST**

| | | |
|---|---|---|
| 31 | Empire Stadium | Vancouver, BC, Canada |
| 30 | Memorial Stadium, Spokane | Spokane, Washington |

**APRIL**

| | | |
|---|---|---|
| 06/05 | Philadelphia Sports Arena | Philadelphia, Pennsylvania |
| 03 | Auditorium | Ottawa, Ontario, Canada |
| 02 | Maple Leaf Gardens | Toronto, Ontario, Canada |
| 01 | Buffalo Memorial Auditorium | Buffalo, New York |

**MARCH**

| | | |
|---|---|---|
| 31 | Olympia Stadium | Detroit, Michigan |
| 30 | Allen County WMC* | Fort Wayne, Texas |
| 29 | Henry W. Kiel Municipal Auditorium | St. Louis, Missouri |
| 28 | International Amphitheater | Chicago, Illinois |

*Typical 1956 set list*

| | |
|---|---|
| Heartbreak Hotel | Blue Suede Shoes |
| I Was the One | Money Honey |
| Long Tall Sally | Hound Dog |
| I've Got a Woman | |

## 1956

### DECEMBER
| | | |
|---|---|---|
| 15 | Hirsch Youth Center | Shreveport, Louisiana |

### NOVEMBER
| | | |
|---|---|---|
| 25 | Jefferson County Armory | Louisville, Kentucky |
| 24 | Hobart Arena | Troy, Ohio |
| 23 | - | Cleveland, Ohio |
| 22 | Toledo Sports Arena | Toledo, Ohio |

### OCTOBER
| | | |
|---|---|---|
| 14 | Freeman Coliseum | San Antonia, Texas |
| 13 | Sam Houston Coliseum | Houston, Texas |
| 12 | Extraco Events Center Fairgrounds | Dallas, Texas |
| 11 | Cotton Bowl | Dallas, Texas |

### SEPTEMBER
| | | |
|---|---|---|
| 26 | Mississippi-Alabama Fairgrounds | Memphis, Tennessee |

### AUGUST
| | | |
|---|---|---|
| 12 | Morris Jeff, Sr. Municipal Auditorium | New Orleans, Louisiana |
| 11/10 | Florida Theater | Jacksonville, Florida |
| 09 | Peabody Auditorium | Orlando, Florida |
| 08 | Municipal Auditorium | Orlando. Florida |
| 06 | Polk Theater | Tampa, Florida |
| 05 | Fort Homer Hesterly Armory | Tampa, Florida |
| 04/3 | Olympia Theatre | Miami, Florida |

### JULY
| | | |
|---|---|---|
| 04 | Russwood Park | Memphis, Tennessee |

### JUNE
| | | |
|---|---|---|
| 30 | The Mosque | Richmond, Virginia |
| 28 | College Park Baseball Field | Columbia, South Carolina |
| 27 | William B. Bell Auditorium | Augusta, Georgia |
| 26 | Charlotte Coliseum | Charlotte, North Carolina |
| 25 | Savannah Sports Arena | Augusta, Georgia |
| 24-22 | Paramount Theater | Atlanta, Georgia |
| 10 | Pima County Rodeo Grounds | Tucson, Arizona |
| 09 | Arizona State Fairgrounds | Phoenix, Arizona |
| 08 | Shrine Auditorium | Los Angeles, California |
| 07 | Riverside Municipal Auditorium | Los Angeles, California |
| 06 | Valley View Casino Center | San Diego, California |
| 03 | Henry J. Kaiser Convention Center | San Francisco, California |

### MAY
| | | |
|---|---|---|
| 27 | Fieldhouse University of Dayton | Dayton, Ohio |
| 26 | Veterans Memorial Auditorium | Columbus, Ohio |
| 25 | Fox Theater | Detroit, Michigan |
| 24 | Municipal Auditorium | Kansas City, Missouri |
| 23 | Municipal Auditorium | Sioux Falls, South Dakota |
| 22 | Veterans Memorial Auditorium | Des Moines, Iowa |
| 21 | Municipal Auditorium | Overland Park, Kansas |
| 20 | Omaha Civic Auditorium | Omaha, Nebraska |
| 19 | University of Nebraska Coliseum | Lincoln, Nebraska |

| | | |
|---|---|---|
| 18 | Wichita Forum | Wichita, Kansas |
| 17 | Shrine Mosque | Springfield, Missouri |
| 16 | Robinson Center Music Hall | Little Rock, Arkansas |
| 15 | Ellis Auditorium (North Music Hall) | Memphis, Tennessee |
| 14 | Mary E. Sawyer Auditorium | Madison, Wisconsin |
| 13 | City Auditorium | Minneapolis, Minnesota |
| 06-01 | New Frontier Hotel | Las Vegas, Nevada |

### APRIL
| | | |
|---|---|---|
| 30-23 | New Frontier Hotel | Las Vegas, Nevada |
| 21 | City Auditorium | Houston, Texas |
| 20 | North Side Convention Center | Dallas, Texas |
| 19 | Municipal Auditorium | Oklahoma City, Oklahoma |
| 18 | Tulsa Fairgrounds Pavilion | Tulsa, Oklahoma |
| 17 | Extraco Events Center-Fairgrounds | Dallas, Texas |
| 16 | Memorial Auditorium | Corpus Christi, Texas |
| 15 | Municipal Auditorium | San Antonio, Texas |
| 13 | Civic Center Auditorium | Amarillo, Texas |
| 12 | Armony | Albuquerque, New Mexico |
| 11 | El Paso | El Paso, Texas |
| 10 | Fair Park Coliseum | Lubbock, Texas |
| 09 | Dallas Memorial Auditorium | Dallas, Texas |
| 08 | Denver Coliseum | Denver, Colorado |
| 05/04 | Valley View Casino Center | San Diego, California |

### MARCH
| | | |
|---|---|---|
| 23 | SS Mt. Vernon Riverboat | Washington D.C. |
| 22 | The Mosque | Richmond, Virginia |
| 21 | YMCA Gymnasium | Winston-Salem, North Carolina |
| 20 | William B. Bell Auditorium | Augusta, Georgia |
| 19 | Township Auditorium | Columbia, South Carolina |
| 18 | County Hall | Columbia, South Carolina |
| 15/14 | Fox Theater | Atlanta, Georgia |

### FEBRUARY
| | | |
|---|---|---|
| 26 | Bayfront Auditorium | Mobile, Alabama |
| 24/23 | Gator Bowl | Jacksonville, Florida |
| 22 | City Auditorium | Waycross, Georgia |
| 21 | Florida Theater | St Petersburg, Florida |
| 20 | Palms Theater | Fort Lauderdale, Florida |
| 19 | Fort Homer, Hesterly Armory | Tampa, Florida |
| 16 | Carolina Theater | Winston-Salem, North Carolina |
| 15 | Williams High School | Burlington, North Carolina |
| 14 | Charles L. Coon High School | Wilson, North Carolina |
| 13 | Paramount Theater | Newport News, Virginia |
| 12 | Montecello Auditorium | Norfolk, Virginia |
| 10/09 | Caroline Theater | Charlotte, North Carolina |
| 08 | Ambassador Theater | Raleigh, North Carolina |
| 07 | Center Theater | Greensboro, North Carolina |
| 06 | National Theater | Greensboro, North Carolina |
| 05 | The Mosque | Richmond, Virginia |

### JANUARY
| | | |
|---|---|---|
| 20 | North Side Coliseum | Dallas, Texas |
| 19 | Kay Bailey Hutchison Conv. Center | Dallas, Texas |
| 18 | The Coliseum | Austin, Texas |

| | | |
|---|---|---|
| 17 | City Auditorium | Houston, Texas |
| 16 | - | Houston, Texas |
| 15 | Municipal Auditorium | San Antonio, Texas |
| 04 | Community Center | Memphis, Tennessee |
| 03 | Von Theatre | Memphis, Tennessee |
| 01 | Henry W. Kiel Municipal Auditorium | St. Louis, Missouri |

## 1955

### DECEMBER

| | | |
|---|---|---|
| 19 | Ellis Auditorium (North Music Hall) | Memphis, Tennessee |
| 12 | National Guard Armory | Amory, Mississippi |

**With Johnny Cash Carl Perkins**

| | | |
|---|---|---|
| 08 | Rialto Theater | Louisville, Kentucky |
| 07/04 | Lyric Theater | Indianapolis, Indiana |
| 03 | Garrett Coliseum | Montgomery, Alabama |
| 02 | Atlanta Civic Arena | Atlanta, Georgia |

### NOVEMBER

| | | |
|---|---|---|
| 25 | Woodrow Wilson Junior | Houston, Texas |
| 19 | Gladewater High School | Gladewater, Texas |
| 18 | Reo Palm Isle Club | Shreveport, Louisiana |
| 17 | Municipal Auditorium | Texarkana, Arkansas |
| 16 | City Auditorium | Camden, Arkansas |
| 15 | Community Center | Sheffield, Alabama |
| 14 | Forrest City High School Auditorium | Forrest City, Arkansas |
| 13 | Ellis Auditorium (North Music Hall) | Memphis, Tennessee |
| 12 | Carthage Milling Co | Carthage, Texas |
| 06 | Community House | Mobile, Alabama |

### OCTOBER

| | | |
|---|---|---|
| 24 | Silver Moon Club | Newport, Arkansas |
| 23-21 | Missouri Theater | St. Louis, Missouri |
| 20 | Brooklyn High School Auditorium | Cleveland, Ohio |
| 19 | Circle Theater | Cleveland, Ohio |
| 17 | Memorial Auditorium | El Dorado, Arkansas |
| 16 | - | Oklahoma City, Oklahoma |
| 15 | Fair Park Coliseum | Lubbock, Texas |
| 14 | - | Lubbock, Texas |
| 13 | Civic Center Auditorium | Amarillo, Texas |
| 11 | Fair Park Auditorium | Dallas, Texas |
| 10 | Soldiers and Sailors Memorial Hall | Brownwood, Texas |
| 08 | City Auditorium | Houston, Texas |
| 06 | Skyline Club | Austin, Texas |
| 05 | Greenville Municipal Auditorium | Dallas, Texas |
| 04 | Boys Club Gymnasium | Paris, Texas |
| 03 | G. Rollie White Coliseum | Houston, Texas |

### SEPTEMBER

| | | |
|---|---|---|
| 22 | Civic Auditorium | Kingsport, Tennessee |
| 21 | Raleigh Memorial Auditorium | Raleigh, North Carolina |
| 20 | Danville-Pittsylvania County Fair | Ringgold, Virginia |
| 19/18 | WRVA Theater | Richmond, Virginia |
| 17 | High School Auditorium | Greensboro, North Carolina |
| 16 | City Auditorium | Knoxville, Tennessee |
| 15 | American Legion Auditorium | Winston-Salem, North Carolina |

| | | |
|---|---|---|
| 14 | Fleming Stadium | Wilson, North Carolina |
| 13 | Shrine Auditorium | Raleigh, North Carolina |
| 12/11 | Norfolk City Auditorium | Norfolk, Virginia |
| 08 | Clarksdale Civic Auditorium | Clarksdale, Mississippi |
| 07 | National Guard Armory | Sikeston, Missouri |
| 06 | Bono High School | Bono, Arkansas |

With Johnny Cash and Carl Perkins

| | | |
|---|---|---|
| 05 | St Francis Country Fair | Forrest City, Arkansas |
| 03 | Round Up Club | Dallas, Texas |
| 02 | Arkansas Municipal Stadium | Texarkana, Arkansas |
| 01 | Pontchartrain Beach | New Orleans, Louisiana |

### AUGUST

| | | |
|---|---|---|
| 26 | Baseball Park | Gonzales, Texas |
| 25 | Sport Center | Austin, Texas |
| 24 | High School Football Field | Conroe, Texas |
| 23 | Saddle Club | Austin, Texas |
| 22 | Spudder Park | Dallas, Texas |
| 12 | Driller Park | Kilgore, Texas |
| 11 | Reo Palm Isle Club | Shreveport, Louisiana |
| 10 | Bear Stadium | Gladewater, Texas |
| 09 | Henderson Rodeo Arena | Henderson, Texas |
| 08 | Mayfair Building | Dallas, Texas |
| 07 | Cook's Hoedown Club | Houston, Texas |
| 06 | River Stadium | Batesville, Arkansas |
| 05 | Overton Park Shell | Memphis, Tennessee |
| 04 | Municipal Auditorium | Camden, Arkansas |
| 03 | Robinson Center Music Hall | Little Rock, Arkansas |
| 02 | Sheffield Community | Muscle Shoals, Alabama |
| 01 | Fairgrounds | Memphis, Tennessee |

### JULY

| | | |
|---|---|---|
| 31 | Fort Homer, Hesterly Armory | Tampa, Florida |
| 30 | Peabody Auditorium | Orlando, Florida |
| 29/28 | Gator Bowl | Jacksonville, Florida |
| 27/26 | Municipal Auditorium | Orlando, Florida |
| 25 | City Auditorium | Cape Coral, Florida |
| 21 | Silver Moon Club | Newport, Arkansas |
| 20 | Cape Arena | St. Louis, Missouri |
| 04 | City Recreation Hall | Stephenville, Texas |
| 03 | Hoedown Club | Corpus Christi, Texas |
| 01 | Casino Club | Baton Rouge, Louisiana |

### JUNE

| | | |
|---|---|---|
| 30/29 | Radio Ranch Club | Mobile, Alabama |
| 28/27 | Air Force Base | Kessler, Mississippi |
| 26 | Slavonian Lodge Auditorium | Mobile, Alabama |
| 24 | - | Altus, Oklahoma City, Oklaho-ma |
| 23 | Southern Club | Oklahoma City, Oklahoma |
| 21 | - | Houston, Texas |
| 20 | - | Houston, Texas |
| 19 | Cook's Hoedown Club | Houston, Texas |
| 18 | Sportarium | Dallas, Texas |
| 17 | Roundup Hall | Stamford, Texas |
| 15 | Belden High School Gymnasium | Belden, North Dakota |

14  Bruce High School Gymnasium — Bruce, Mississippi
10  American Legion Hall — Breckenridge, Texas
08  Auditorium — Sweetwater, Texas
05  Hope Parks & Rec. Center Coliseum — Hope, Arkansas
03  Fair Park Coliseum — Lubbock, Texas
01  High School Auditorium — Guymon, Oklahoma

## MAY

31  High School Field House — Lubbock, Texas
29/28  Sportarium — Dallas, Texas
26  Junior College Stadium — Jackson, Mississippi
25  American Legion Hall — Jackson, Mississippi
22  Cook's Hoedown Club — Houston, Texas
19  Raleigh Memorial Auditorium — Duke Raleigh, North Carolina
18  American Legion Auditorium — Winston-Salem, North Carolina
17  City Auditorium — Knoxville, Tennessee
16  The Mosque — Richmond, Virginia
15  Norfolk City Auditorium — Norfolk, Virginia
14  Shrine Auditorium — Raleigh, North Carolina
13/12  Gator Bowl — Jacksonville, Florida
10  Southeastern Pavilion — Orlando, Florida
09  City Auditorium — Cape Coral, Florida
08  Fort Homer Hesterly Armory — Tampa, Florida
07  Peabody Auditorium — Orlando, Florida
05/04  Ladd Peebles Stadium — Mobile, Alabama
02  High School Auditorium — Baton Rouge, Louisiana
01  Morris Jeff, Sr, Municipal Auditorium — New Orleans, Louisiana

## APRIL

30  Gladewater High School — Gladewater, Texas
**With Jim Reeves, Johnny Horton, Slim Whitman and Scotty Moore**
29  Cotton Club — Lubbock, Texas
**With Johnny Cash, Carl Perkins and Buddy Holly**
26  City Auditorium — Big Spring, Texas
25  High School Auditorium — Seymour, Texas
24  Cook's Hoedown Club — Houston, Texas
23  Extraco Events Center-Fair — Dallas, Texas
22  Arkansas Municipal Stadium — Texarkana, Arkansas
20  American Legion Hut — Grenada, Mississippi
16  Sportarium — Dallas, Texas
15  Stamford High School — Stamford, Texas
13  High School Auditorium — Breckenridge, Texas
10  Cook's Hoedown Club — Houston, Texas
07  Court Meeting House — Corinth, Mississippi
02  City Auditorium — Houston, Texas
01  Ector County Auditorium — Lubbock, Texas

## MARCH

31  Reo Palm Isle Club — Shreveport, Louisiana
30  El Dorado High School Auditorium — El Dorado, Arkansas
20  Cook's Hoedown Club — Houston, Texas
19  Eagles Hall — Houston, Texas
10  Clarksdale Civic Auditorium — Clarksdale, Mississippi
09  Armony Concert Hall — Memphis, Tennessee
08  Catholic Club — Helena-West Helena, Arkansas
04  High School — Dekalb, Texas

02  Armory — Newport, Arkansas

## FEBRUARY

26  Circle Theater — Cleveland, Ohio
25  City Auditorium — Texarkana, Arkansas
24  South Side Elementary School — Bastrop, Louisiana
23  Watson Chapel High School — Little Rock, Arkansas
22  City Hall — Hope, Arkansas
21  City Auditorium — Camden, Arkansas
20  Robinson Center Music Hall — Little Rock, Arkansas
18  West Monroe High School — West Monroe, Louisiana
17  City Auditorium — Lubbock, Texas
16  Senior High School Field House — Lubbock, Texas
15  Fair Park Auditorium — Dallas, Texas
14  North Junior High School — Roswell, New Mexico
13  Cotton Club — Lubbock, Texas
12  American Legion Hall — Carlsbad, New Mexico
11  Carlsbad Sports Arena — Carlsbad, New Mexico
10  High School Auditorium — Alpine, Texas
07  Ripley High Gymnasium — Ripley, Mississippi
06  Ellis Auditorium (North Music Hall) — Memphis, Tennessee
04  Golden Cadillac Club — New Orleans, Louisiana

## JANUARY

28  Gaston High School Auditorium — Gaston, Texas
27  Reo Palm Isle Club — Shreveport, Louisiana
26  Rural Electrification Building — Gilmer, Texas
25  Mayfair Building — Dallas, Texas
24  Recreation Hall, Humble Oil Camp — Hawkins, Texas
21  National Guard Armory — Sikeston, Missouri
20  - — Leachville, Arkansas
19  Community Centre — Sheffield, Alabama
18  Acorn Country Courthouse — Corinth, Mississippi
17  Northeast Mississippi Comm College — Booneville, Mississippi
14  - — Marianna, Arkansas
13  Catholic Club — Helena-West Helena, Arkansas
12  Clarksdale Civic Auditorium — Clarksdale, Mississippi
07  Midland High School — Lubbock, Texas
06  Cotton Club — Lubbock, Texas
05  City Auditorium — Lubbock, Texas
04  Odessa High School Auditorium — Lubbock, Texas
01  Eagles Hall — Houston, Texas

## 1949

## MAY

25  Kansas Coliseum — Wichita, Kansas

*concertarchives.org

# The Blue Moon Boys Interviews

## Interview with DJ Fontana

I met Scotty, Bill and Elvis at the Louisiana hayride down in Shreveport, Louisiana. I had heard their records, they were playing rock in that one area and one of the managers called me there one day and said "I want you to listen to this record". So I went to his office and they played it and I said How many guys they got playing in this band?" and they said" Just 3 guys" and it sounded like 5 or 6 people with the echo and everything and I said "Boy that's awfully good."

So anyway, they come in and Scotty said "would you like to work with those tonight?" and I said "Yeah, well that's why I'm here" so I said "Let's go back into the dressing room and kind of talk about it". So Elvis got his guitar and Scotty and Bill and they just played a little bit and I said "Yeah, we can do that then". So we did it that night and he'd come back in a few weeks later and we did it again. Two or three weeks and he'd come back in and out. So that's how it basically got started. Just by accident I happened to be there.

**Q. What were your first impressions of Elvis as a musician, what did you make of him?**

Well, his voice was so unusual for that time period and his clothes were unusual – his dress with the peg pants and all that stuff and stripes down his pants leg. And he was a good looking kid, a good looking guy and I said "Hey this guy might do ok – who knows?" he had that certain charisma about him that there was no way for him to miss, no way.

**Q. What was the music scene like then? Was Elvis ahead of his time?**

Yeah, well I think he was a little bit ahead of his time. We were all still listening to the big bands – Woody Herman, Stan Kenton, those kinds of guys. The Dorsey Brothers – that's all we had basically on radio. They had a couple of blues stations but they didn't get out very far – 5,000 miles and stuff like that and so we were really into the big band listening.

**Q. What kind of drummer are you yourself? Where did you get a lot of your influences?**

From the big bands, listening to those guys play and watching them, if they'd come in town. Sometimes every now and again there would be a big orchestra come through town on a one nighter. And we'd all go out and see them play and you learn a little bit from each one of the guys.

**Q. How did it feel going from behind the curtain to in front of the curtain?**

Oh it was different yeah it was just a farce I think. Basically the country acts and the country programmes wasn't really for me with drums at all. So they weren't sure how the people would take us so they'd say "Well you stand back there and play" and I'd say "Well that's alright with me" you get paid the same money you know. And every couple of weeks they'd say "Well, just bring a snare drum out and bring a cymbal out" and by the time we'd got through with Elvis they had the whole set out he said "Just bring them all out".That's what he wanted and that's what Elvis wanted so I guess maybe they kind of figured they'd better go along with his wishes I guess cos he was drawing a lot of people in there by then.

**Q. So obviously what you were used to was different from what Elvis was playing? What kind of music was being played, where was the influence coming from?**

I think they'd come from a lot of black groups being from a Memphis area and he'd listened to a lot of black radio programmes. Scotty was a kind of a blues, jazz player he wanted to be and Bill was just an all-round bass player, that's not country not pop just, the feel of that's what he did, he had good feeling to his bass playing.

**Q. What kind of drums were you using? What kind of sound were you trying to achieve?**

Well I had Gretsch drums and so that's all I really knew, what they sounded like and I used them on all the early

can't answer those questions whatsoever. I thought that since he had to go to Vegas, he needed a show band, I mean he needed a production and that's what they were looking for and that's why he went over so well in Vegas.

**Q. American Trilogy – the ultimate Elvis song do you think?**

I think so, I like that song myself. Micky Newberry did a great job on it and Elvis sung the fire out of it. A lot of people out there in the audience, you'd see them on that split screen and you could see these people out there crying cos he was very sincere about it.

**Q. Do the early 70s films of Elvis in concert do him justice as a performer?**

Oh yeah, that's when he really got into the karate moves and the kicks and the big bands behind him and he really sounded good with that big band, he really did.

**Q. Do you think Elvis was a perfectionist in terms of his performance?**

Oh yeah, he wanted everything exactly right. Even on his records he wanted it right. He'd say "No we have to do it again".You gotta remember way back then we only had mono tracks so there weren't no fixing nothing, you'd go back in and do the whole song again so we just kept going.

**Q. Aloha from Hawaii – the best example of a mature Elvis in concert?**

That was another great concert but you know it's hard to say which one was the best cos there were all good. They made darn sure that he did a good job, course he made sure that he did a good job and the sound was good and the film was good and they all did great job – I can't say a darn thing bad about it.

**Q. Do you think the 70s Vegas repertoire was sufficiently challenging?**

No, no, he was doing basically his old songs except different tempos and I think he threw away a lot of the vocals on those up tempo when it got so fast that nobody

could understand what he was talking about half of the time. I think he should have done them originally where they were and do more of them if he had to but don't just rush through them. No I don't think that's a good idea.

**Q. Could the effect of Elvis' decline in health be seen in his later performances?**

Well I didn't see him after a while anyhow. I knew that like everyone else you read the papers and you knew he was sick here and he was sick there. It seemed like every time he'd come to town he'd get sick and he ended up in the hospital and there was always something back and forth, it wasn't anything serious but it was just enough to figure he had been kind of not real well for the last few years.

**Q. I mean, were drugs a problem when you worked with him?**

No, never saw them. In fact he didn't drink. Me, Scotty and Bill, we'd have a beer or two you know and that was about it.

**Q. Do you think Elvis was overrated or is he really the King in your opinion?**

No he wasn't overrated by no means. He didn't like to be called the King but still he was the number 1 guy and he still is. I just got back from Denmark and Sweden and there's people over there that still love Elvis. Everywhere you go they love Elvis, after all these years he's passed away.

**Q. Do you remember where you were and how you felt when you heard he'd passed away?**

I was at Sun Records actually, not Memphis but over at Belmont and Shelby Singleton had brought all this stuff out, all the Sun stuff and we were cutting somebody over there I don't remember who it was now and he came on the talkback about 4-4.30. He said "DJ" he said "We just heard Elvis had passed away" and he said "It's on the radio" he said "You want to call the session?"We were supposed to be through at 5 anyhow. I said "No, let's finish up". Costs a lot of money just to cancel a session you know, I said "No, no, we'll wait till 5 and then I'll run home". I didn't live too far from the studio at the time, maybe 10 minutes away. And I got on the phone and I tried to call everybody I knew, that was associated with Elvis at that time. Couldn't get any, everybody was out of pocket. Everybody was either in the air coming or going. So finally I got hold of Joe Esposito at the house finally and he said it's true. So I caught the next plane out the next morning, me and my wife and the kids we went down and spent the whole day with them you know, at the home and the next morning I had to leave actually I had to go to Virginia – I had some more sessions up there so Billy Smith took me out the back gate, and back to the airport, me and the family and I got back home that night about 10 or 11 o'clock, so it was a sad, sad day for everybody.

**Q. To sum up, is there anything you'd like to add about the whole time you were with Elvis and the whole time you were in the band?**

Well the only thing is like I said, early on we all had a great time together. And I think the reason for that was we could all talk and sleep in the cars, stop and get a hamburger if you wanted to so that made it a little easier. As he got bigger and bigger and bigger, well we could feel that as we got bigger we couldn't get in the venues as easy.

We had to have certain passes, certain security and all that stuff. And it made it hard for everybody and we only saw him actually on stage and he's off stage. But early on it was all driving and stopping for food and one thing and another, we had a lot of time to talk.

## Interview With Scotty Moore

**Q. Tell me about when you first picked up the guitar, when you were in the Navy – tell me about your influences?**

Well I guess I started trying to play a little bit when I was around 9 or 10 years old, I got interested in it. I had three brothers, my three brothers and my dad all played string instruments and there was 14 years difference between me and the next one up the ladder. And so by the time I got to that age, everybody was gone, married or in the navy or whatever and I think one thing drove me was just being hard headed more than anything else

**Q. And what kind of music were you interested in?**

Any kind, it didn't matter. Course I heard a lot of country music back, coming off the farm and a lot of black music and I heard some popular music of course on the radio and stuff like that.

**Q. You have quite a unique style. How did you develop that unique style?**

Just stealing from everybody I guess and putting it all together. If I've got a style – I never considered that I did. I tried to play the song, I tried to listen to the song cos I don't read music or at least as Chet Atkins used to say "You didn't read enough to hurt your playing." I tried to listen to a song and play something I'd think would fit the music or the way the guy was singing, you know, that way.

**Q. When did you first get involved with working with Elvis? When did you first meet him and what were your first impressions of him?**

Well I had a group of my own in Memphis called The Starlite Wranglers, which I had formed right after I had got out of the navy and we did one record at Sun and, when I found out there was a place there where you could make records, I went in and talked to Sam Phillips. He agreed to listen to the group and we went in and auditioned for him and at first, I always remember, the first thing he said was "Have you got any original material?" and we said "No." And he said "Well you got a good group, I like the group.

If you get some original material, come back, I'd like to see what you got."And so me and my oldest brother and Doug Poindexter, we wrote 2 songs just over a few days and we went back and we did the record with Sam which he put out and we sold maybe 10 or 12, one of those kind of deals, but from all that Sam and I became good friends.

The job I had I was through work probably 2 or 3 o'clock in the afternoon and I'd drive by the studio and if he wasn't tied up working well we'd go next door to Miss Taylor's restaurant and drink coffee and just chit chat about the business and "What do you think?" and "What do you think we need to do?" just in general and one day we were having coffee and his secretary was there, Miss Marion

Keisker was with us and she asked Sam "Did you ever talk to that boy that was in here about a year ago that cut that demo for his mother's .." she gave the details and he said "No."

So I'd say about probably a week or two went by and every day that went by and I saw him and be there having coffee together I'd always ask him "Oh by the way did you ever contact that boy?" cos I kept that in my mind.

So finally one day Marion again was having coffee with us and he turned to her and asked her and... I said "I haven't even heard this guy's name yet, even", and he turned to Marion and says "Get that guy, have you still got his telephone number?" She says "Yeah" and he said "Give it to Scotty" and he turned to me and said "You call him and ask him to come over to your house and see what you think." And that was fine. So in a little bit Marion goes and comes back and gives me the piece of paper with his number on it and I looked at it and I say "His name – Elvis Presley – what kind of a name is that?" And that was really all that was said and goodbye.

When I got home that afternoon I called and his mother answered and she said that he was at the theatre I believe and that she'd have him call when he got back. So a couple of hours later he called and I told him that I was working with Sam Phillips and he was looking for material, looking for artists blah, blah and would he be interested in doing an audition and he said "Well sure."

And I asked him to come over to my house, which was on Bill's Avenue, the next day which was July the, Sunday would have been the 4th, no 3rd, no 4th cos Memphis didn't shoot fireworks on Sunday but Sunday they did actually celebrate it on next day on Monday, that's the way it went.

He came over that Sunday and he sat around and he played and sang everything, it seemed like he knew every song in the world and, but he didn't know how to play half of them. But he'd play along and when he didn't know the chords he'd just keep playing, keep singing. And this went on for a couple of hours. Bill Black at that time, he lived just a few doors down the street from me and he came down to sit in, just listening with us for a little while and left. Then when Elvis left I told Elvis I said "Either I or Sam will probably be calling you about coming into the studio".

I called Sam and I told him I said "Well it seems like the boy knows all the songs. Being as young as he is he's got a good voice", and Sam said "Well I'll call him and ask him to come in tomorrow night", which would have been Monday night and said "Can you and Bill come in and do a little background? I don't want the whole band, I just need a little noise behind him to see what he sounds like".

And we said "Sure." Bill came back down and I asked Bill, I said "Bill what did you think of him?" And he said "Alright - seems like a new bunch of songs, he sounds pretty good you know? Had good timing", and so forth, that kind of thing. And so we went down to the studio the next night, Monday night and there again, he went through all these different songs, just whatever came to mind, Sam didn't request anything or anything. It was at least 10 o'clock, it was getting late, we were about ready to go to the house cos it was still just an audition.

And Elvis stood up and started playing his guitar and singing That's Alright and Bill started slapping his bass and playing along with him. I had never heard the song, Bill had never heard it and I took the guitar and started playing, looking for something, we were just jamming.

The door to the control room was open and Sam stuck his head out and said "What are you guys doing?" We said "we're just goofing around" and he said "Well just do it a little more". Cos the mics weren't on or anything and he said "Let me go and turn the mics on" or whatever and we got on the mic, went through it 2 or 3 times and that was it. Lord am I glad or am I sorry, I don't know!

**Q. So tell me a bit about The Blue Moon Boys and your fellow musicians Bill and DJ?**

Well Blue Moon Boys was just Bill and myself. They dropped that name when we left Sun. DJ never recorded with us. We started using DJ when we went to the Louisiana Hayride and he did a lot of shows with us during the period we were on Sun.

Heartbreak Hotel was the first thing he played on when we came to Nashville to RCA.

**Q. Did the phenomenon with rock and roll happen overnight or did it slowly happen?**

Well, actually the first thing is – what is rock and roll? Alan Freed had a disc jockey show up in, where was he? He was the one that coined that phrase. I suppose everybody knows really what the term really means – it came from black music and they would use that term to get across their message. I don't know, that name did stick when he started calling it rock and roll. Before that Elvis was being called the Hillbilly Cat, Rockabilly – gosh I don't know what else they called him.

I'm sure he had some good names. But for us, as far as the band, we just enjoyed playing – there wasn't a producer, there wasn't somebody who said you gotta play something this way or that way – they let us do what we wanted to do.

**Q. What happened after that? Did you start working with Elvis full time? When did you also become his manager?**

Well the first thing, the group I was telling you about that I had, The Starlite Wranglers, we were doing a Friday and Saturday gig at a small club here in town, Bel Air Club, and that was the first thing after we cut That's Alright – then a few days went by and we finally came up with the B-side and that came up in really the same way, cos we went back in a couple of days later and Elvis started going through all different songs.

Sam would think of something or I would think of something and he'd try it "Do you know so and so?" "Yeah I know it" – and he'd try something else.

Bill was sitting on his bass fiddle, I don't know, if you have a bass just laying on the floor and he was sitting, just sitting on it and he started beating on it and singing Blue Moon of Kentucky which was a waltz country song by Bill Monroe and he was singing it in falsetto, high tenor you know, up tempo and Elvis knew the song and he started singing along with him. That was the B side, it was that simple.

**Q. When you were in the studio, how many takes would it take to do songs?**

Well, once we landed on something that he knew and liked, it might have been something that Sam had put out before or whatever – but when he liked the song and everything, well it didn't take us too long. He might miss a word, I might miss a chord, Sam would goof sometimes when we were recording, but we're talking about skin of your teeth back in those days, but once we'd got everything in order, it didn't take too many takes. It was just mainly – when he was satisfied that he'd done his best singing, it was the main thing.

**Q. Was he a perfectionist?**

It was the feel, he wanted to feel, we all felt the same way, if I might have missed a note or not hit a note perfect, if the total thing felt good, that's what counted.

I mean I might have played something fantastic and I would never have played the same thing twice anyway but when I played if it felt good, it was the same thing. Elvis was the same way.

**Q. Can you tell us a bit about where we are now?**

Well, we're in RCAB in Nashville. We cut a few things here. Course I guess most of our recording was done in California and some of the hits were done, a few were done in New York too. But all the time I was with him, we did several of them here.

**Q. Tell us about how you became his manager and what that relationship was like?**

Well after we put out that first record, of course the local DJs around Memphis started getting calls and everything. A couple of other people that were "music managers" and what have you and everybody was calling him. The three of us – Bill, Sam, myself and Elvis - were all just sitting chatting one day and he was talking about the people calling him and he said "Well I don't know what to tell them". And it was actually Sam's idea he said "Well I'll tell you what.

Scotty, why don't you sign up as manager for a year and it'll give us time to look for somebody that we all trust and want to work with."And that's the way it happened and of course, we had Bob Neil came in, who was a local disc jockey and he started booking us in and around Memphis, Arkansas, Mississippi, locally – cos he was on a radio station, I think he was on about 6 o'clock in the morning and at that time in the morning the station really went out.

**Q. What was life on the road like?**

Starting off like that, none of us had ever been on the road so number one you'd have an experience and then pretty soon you'd start to get tired and say will this never end. And yet tomorrow the next show will be better, there'll be a better show, there'll be more money, it'll be, you know, everything is supposed to go up. But we were just typical, like, I won't say like any other band that's out there but – we'd have our fusses and everything. Bill and I did most of the driving in the early days then when DJ joined us, he did some of the driving too.

We had a problem with Elvis when he was driving – he was a good driver, a very good driver – but for some reason he just could not read road signs. If you came to a fork in the road, well, he'd take the wrong one every time. But he was a good driver. DJ was a good driver. We were on the road when they were just starting to build interstates and we left Memphis going – I don't know where we were going – but, we got to St Louis where they had just built the brand new ring road around, and it was around 11 o'clock at night or something like that.

I had been driving and I turned it over to DJ and got over in the other seat and went to sleep. Bill and Elvis were in the back seat. I woke up in daylight, sitting on the side of the road, still asleep and I said "Where are we at?" and he says "Still in St Louis." He said "I can't get off this damn road."We never let him forget it either. He'll probably bring it up.

**Q. What was the music scene like when you went to the live events?**

In the very, very, very early days when Bob Naylor was booking us, we were doing a lot of little country schoolhouses, I say country schoolhouses cos they were little towns and the schoolhouses would be outside of the city limits maybe. And say the show was starting at 7 o'clock we would get there at 7.30 and there wouldn't be a

soul anywhere. And you had to take your own PAs – I mean they had PAs in those little places like that, it was just had a microphone that sometimes just plugged into my little amplifier. There wasn't even any equipment there – you'd take all of that.

We were the whole show and we started getting some other people to go with us. Arnie Wheeler was a country artist back then – he went with us on a lot. But anyway, we would get there about 7.30, and get set up, 8 o'clock doors open and just whoof! everybody was there.

Well, they'd heard the record on the radio but they hadn't seen him. And they were just sitting.Well Bill started cutting up cos the bass player back in those days, especially on country acts, the bass player always had to dress up in, be a clown but he started whooping and hollering, sitting on the bass, riding the bass and just cutting up you know.

And the people would start coming alive by watching him and then they would get into the music and that's what really got him started. I mean he, and everything he'd do, they'd clap andcarry on and he'd embellish on it.

**Q. And had he always had those dance moves and the lip snarl or did that come later?**

The only thing that he had natural that I know of was the first thing we did at the Overton Park Shell that was the first actual stage performance in front of an audience and Bob Naylor got us on that as a closing, actually as an extra act – Slim Whitman was the featured singer on that.

And for me the guitar player, if he's standing up, usually will either pat his foot, keep in time or sit down and if he doesn't do it he doesn't do anything. But Elvis, when he was singing and playing he'd always raise up on the balls of his feet, both feet. And with the big breeches legs back then, they started flapping and he looked like he was really getting going with it. And that was what they were really laughing about, going on about.

**Q. Is there any myths you want to dispel about anything that's out there in the media?**

If you could name them, I could tell you a whole bunch of

them but they just don't come right to mind.

**Q. I had June 27th – was that another meeting?**

July 4th was the first day I met him – I talked to him on the phone the day before. Of course I found out much later that he had been in Sun before and had done some of those little demos supposedly for his mother. But he had never mentioned that.

**Q. So when was the turning point where Sun and RCA came in there? When did that change?**

There was '54/'55 were the Sun sessions, we discussed those.

**Q. When did you guys go from Sun to RCA?**

Well, there had been several people trying to buy us contracts and Parker came into the deal and set the whole thing up with RCA and they paid Sam the money. And this was when we went to RCA and cut the first record.

**Q. And can you tell us a bit about that?**

Well, it was just another studio date we did it at Trafco. Their building was down on McGavock Street and in the lower floor RCA had rented the studio and that's where we cut Heartbreak Hotel.

**Q. Tell me, what were your feelings about Colonel Parker and that change in management? What did you make of that?**

Well, I probably don't want to get into that.

**Q. OK, tell me about the movies. I heard you were in a couple of the movies. What did you make of the soundtracks?**

We did a couple of the early ones with him as extras. Well it was actually the band in one, the first one – I always say the first one, we weren't in – that was interesting.We went out to – when he did Love Me Tender – they took The Jordanaires, Bill, DJ, myself and Elvis they had us all come out to a bungalow on the lot at MGM and it was all pre set-

up, we knew that later, cos Elvis didn't know anything either about it.

You've seen the movie, you know what it was about. So we go into our regular show we're doing on the tour. And they said "No that's not the kind of music we want, sorry." "That was ok thank you very much". Then we see the movie and we've been playing hillbilly music all our lives. But it was set up – Ken Derby, who was the musical director, he had his own guys he wanted to use. I understand those kind of things. It wasn't bad, you just knew it was pre-done.

**Q. What did you make of Elvis as an actor?**

I just wish he could have got some real scripts later on. When they found out they could make some money off of him, I guess, well, he went ahead and did it – I never will understand why. He just wouldn't put his foot down on management and say "I will not do this. Give me something." He did have a chance at A Star is Born – they had that in mind for him, and then Parker wouldn't let him do it.

**Q. What did you think of Elvis as a person?**

Well, he was just a regular guy. With all the stuff that hit him at such an early age and so fast - he never really had a chance to grow up. He always had his so-called friends around him and he just never grew up.

**Q. Cos I was going to ask you about the money, it's fascinating, but if you don't want to talk about it?**

That happened here by the way. Yes, he cut that song here in...... yeah, I think Jerry Reed wrote and played on.

**Q. Do you think that early on drugs were affecting Elvis in the early years?**

It didn't affect his music really at the time that I was with him. He didn't really get into that, that started when he was in the army, he started taking binnies. I think they used to give them when they were going out on manoeuvres because he was driving a tank. It used to keep you awake and that was the normal thing. But I guess he got to liking them pretty good and then went onto different stuff. I don't know really all the background on that just what I read.

**Q. What did you think of The Jordanaires and what did they bring to the Elvis sound?**

What can you say, when he found a group he liked and he liked The Jordanaires from even before he'd ever recorded with them so it was just natural that they would work with him. They still sound good, you know.

**Q. Where do you think Elvis got a lot of his influence?**

Mostly from religion music. He loved quartets, he loved The Jordanaires, The Blackwood Brothers, just the way he was raised, he used to go to all night singings and such. I guess that's where he first met The Jordanaires maybe – he met them in Memphis - they were there on a show I think.

**Q. What about your guitars, what did you use back then?**

On the first record I had an ES-295, Gibson ES-295. And when I first came out of the navy I bought a Fender and, mainly because in the navy there were a couple of other guys on there who played a little bit, and we'd bought Japanese guitars when going to port and the

frets were made out of beer cans cos you'd wear the frets out in 30 days. But we were always sitting down so they were thin guitars, like Fenders, call them copies of Fenders.

And when I came out I bought a Fender but then standing up I couldn't keep it still, it kept getting away from me. And I was walking down town one day by the music store and they had just put one of the ES-295s in there which was gold coloured and all the hardware was gold-plated and everything and I said "I gotta have it."

And I went in and made a trade and got that, and that's what I had when we first got started. I kept it through the first 4 records.

On the 5th record I got an EchoSonic amplifier which had an echo in it that, I'd heard this on one record by Chet Atkins and my thought was that if I had that – cos I was always worried we'd do something and when Sam was using the slapback echo on the whole song, that when we

went out to do the show it would sound lah, you know, it didn't have the pep then.

And I knew that if I could get that amplifier then at least one instrument would have the right sound. And I called Nashville and I don't remember who I talked to now but I found out somehow or another from chat that Ray Butts was in Cairo, Illinois, a music store that had designed this amp and I drove up there to see him and he said "Yeah, be glad to build you one." Now this is 1954 and it only cost $500 for that amplifier. I still have it.

**Q. Shake, Rattle and Roll – was this the world's first glimpse of Elvis?**

Yeah, probably so. They might have heard the name. Yeah.

**Q. Hound Dog – can you describe what made the early Elvis sound unique in musical terms?**

There again, we just did what we felt. We only had 3 Jordanaires on that. Gordon Stoker was playing piano cos Shorty Long had another gig he had to go to he was working on a stage show and so he had to leave. And Gordon took over piano and so we just had the 3 Jordanaires singing on that. And you can tell it if you listen to it real close with a musical ear. I'm trying to be real nice about Tez. But let me interject this, when everything got that it felt good for everybody, that was the cut.

**Q. Do you think the early television performances were good in musical terms?**

No, because they could have been so much better, you weren't allowed to, you couldn't set a mike in front, you couldn't dare see a microphone then or anything, the mike was probably way up in the air. You know how television used to be. Now they finally got away from that – ok, you're playing the guitar or what, let me see it.

**Q. They used to put the drummer behind the curtain?**

Yeah, oh yeah. DJ used to play at the Hayride, that's when we first met him – he was playing behind a screen. There was a shadow, you could see the shadow but you didn't see him. Now you don't wanna see him!

**Q. Do you think the guitar breaks were important in the early arrangements?**

Well, I don't know if they would have been important or not. They were just of the style of the day, as it has always been. A singer will sing a verse or two, then whether it's the guitar or a piano or whatever it is then the instrumental pad goes in there too. Better leave that up to the beholding of the people listening I guess.

**Q. Was there anything out of the ordinary in Elvis' version of Blue Suede Shoes and Tutti Frutti that was better than the original renditions?**

Just that we did them probably faster maybe.Again we just did it the way we felt it. RCA, Steve Scholes whatever had been trying to get, when Carl's record was doing real good, they'd been trying to get Elvis to cover it and Elvis wouldn't do it. He said "No, I'm not going to cover it, cos Carl's a friend of mine, we work the shows together", and so forth. We were going to New York, I can't remember which show we were going to be on. But Carl had one also up there and they'd had, that's when Carl had the wreck and Bill, DJ and myself were on our way up to there.

We went by to see Carl in the hospital and they all said send him a telegram or call in with something also. But he was already in New York. And when we got to New York he said he wanted to do Blue Suede Shoes on the show. He was doing it for Carl, you know, he wasn't trying to take away anything. Cos they had been pushing him trying to get him to do it before Carl had the wreck.

**Q. Do you think Heartbreak Hotel was the first real Elvis classic?**

Well, yeah cos it was the first record on RCA and of course it had been the first one that was played all over the whole country. Before that it was strictly a southern regional hit kind of thing.

**Q. And Suspicious Minds – was this the perfect repertoire for Elvis? Did it sum up what was happening in his life at the time?**

No, I never thought of it that way. I don't know. Could be.

**Q. American Trilogy – the ultimate Elvis song?**

See that was done originally by Micky Newberry. Elvis had heard it. I think he believed it was just a good show tune to do on stage and maybe make some people stand up straighter and salute or so – political type thing you know.

**Q. Do you think he was a perfectionist in terms of his performances, Elvis?**

Well a perfectionist you never knew what he was going to do. I mean when he went on stage you didn't know what he was going to do. There was perfection maybe in his own way and how he was going to do something but we didn't know what he was going to do.

**Q. Could the effect of Elvis' decline in health be seen in his later performances do you think?**

Well, the only time I saw him was when he was on video or something. The last time I saw him, I can't remember what the show was, where he had gained so much weight and I could tell there was something wrong but I didn't know what.

**Q. Can you remember where you were when he passed away and what your feelings were?**

Yeah, I was in the control room at Monument Studios doing some editing as such.

**Q. And how did you feel?**

I don't know, well I guess just saddened of course.

**Q. Do you think Elvis is overrated or do you think he's the king?**

He wouldn't have liked the title king, I know that for sure. If we could break everything down, he would be underrated in some things and he'd be overrated in other things. So I'd just leave that to the individual.

**Q. What about the book? Can you mention anything about the book and how that came about?**

Jim Dickerson was the one that did the book on me. He'd just been pestering me to do it and I finally gave in – that's all I know.

**Q. Did your daughter have something to do with that?**

Yeah, our daughter was friends of his and that came about in a roundabout way, Vicky.

**Q. Is there anything you might like to add?**

No I'm fine if you've got enough. The book had been out of print for some time but they've done another printing and brought it up to date, added another chapter about all my illnesses and hospital stays and such mostly.

**Q. Are you ok now?**

Yeah, I got a couple of nice holes in my head. I guess so.

**Q. Do you pick up the guitar now?**

Yeah, I still try to play a little bit. I'm still having trouble with my right arm and hand but part of that's just pure age, arthritis.

**Q. And if I were to say that your guitar playing was a major role in the history of American popular music, what would you say?**

Thank you!

Elvis showing framed gold record of Heartbreak Hotel to (L-R) drummer D.J. Fontana, singer Gordon Stoker and guitarist Scotty Moore, 1956